Praise for
The Happiness Makeover

"M.J. Ryan is a wonderful guid
the art and science of being tru
her experience, and her vulnerability and sincerity are
infectious. After reading this inspiring and informative
book, you'll know the best ideas and methods for creating
a delicious and delightful life."

—Jonathan Robinson, author of *Find Happiness Now*
and *Communication Miracles for Couples*

"This book is like happy electricity—connecting us all to
our joy, which we continually forget how to access."

—SARK, author/artist of
Make Your Creative Dreams Real

"A wonderful blend of motivation, inspiration, and expla-
nation, *The Happiness Makeover* is a recipe for enjoying
today and all your tomorrows."

—David Niven, PhD, author of
The 100 Simple Secrets of Happy People

"Happiness is at the fingertips of every person on the planet. In *The Happiness Makeover*, M. J. Ryan provides example after example of people learning how to choose happiness. She offers wisdom from the ages and provides practical insights and advice on how you, too, can achieve happiness right now. A fun and enlightening book."

—Barry Neil Kaufman, author of *Happiness Is a Choice* and co-founder of the Option Institute

"While we all want to be happy, we're not always sure that we know what happiness is or how to have more if it. This wonderful book answers both questions. It's based on the wisdom of the ages, and is informative, upbeat, and a delight to read. Keep it handy."

—Hal Urban, author of *Life's Greatest Lessons*

THE
HAPPINESS
MAKEOVER

THE
HAPPINESS
MAKEOVER

Overcome Stress and Negativity
to Become a Hopeful, Happy Person

M. J. RYAN

Conari Press

Published by Conari Press, a division of Mango Publishing Group, Inc.

Cover Design: Elina Diaz
Layout Design: Jane Hagaman

For permission requests, please contact the publisher at:
Mango Publishing Group
2850 S Douglas Road, 4th Floor
Coral Gables, FL 33134 USAinfo@mango.bz

For special orders, quantity sales, course adoptions and corporate sales, please email the publisher at sales@mango.bz. For trade and wholesale sales, please contact Ingram Publisher Services at customer.service@ingramcontent.com or +1.800.509.4887.

The Happiness Makeover: Overcome Stress and Negativity to Become a Hopeful, Happy Person

Library of Congress Cataloging-in-Publication Data is available on request.
ISBN: (p) 978-1-64250-927-4 (e) 978-1-64250-928-1
BISAC category code HEA055000, HEALTH & FITNESS / Mental Health

Printed in the United States of America

"Remember happiness doesn't depend
upon who you are or what you have;
it depends solely on what you think."

—*Dale Carnegie*

Contents

III
ACTIVATING DAILY HAPPINESS / 66

IV
TWENTY-TWO INSTANT
HAPPINESS BOOSTERS / 170

V
LOVING YOUR LIFE / 178

I
YOU CAN BE HAPPIER

"What would happen to us if we really fell in love with life? How would our lives change if we really thought... that reality is fabulous... ? Would we be fools of whom other people take advantage, or would we find that life is exciting, joyful, and wonderful?"

—*James A. Kitchens*

It was a cold, dreary Saturday morning. My husband and I had plans to go out to dinner for a joint birthday celebration. Then Ana, our then three-year-old, woke up with a fever. She'd had recurring pneumonia since we adopted her at age one and fever was the warning sign. Cancel the sitter and hunker down to deal with one crabby child. For a sick Ana was not a pleasant experience—she'd cling to me and scream bloody murder if Don or anyone else came close.

Somehow we survived the day, but not without many tears and tantrums. As night fell, I had her in my lap in the rocking chair. "Hard day, huh Ana," I said. "What was going on? What do you want?"

She looked up at me and wailed, "I just want to be happy."

Don't we all? No matter who we are or what our circumstances, isn't that what we each long for? Happiness, the experience of the sheer joy of being alive. Indeed, it is such an important shared value that the Declaration of Independence identifies its pursuit as one of only three unalienable rights.

We all want it so badly, but like Ana on that December day, so many of us don't seem to know how to experience it on a consistent basis. Maybe the problem is with the word "pursue." Somehow we've gotten the message that happiness is out there, something to be sought after—in the right job, the mate who never annoys you, the $50,000 BMW—rather than inside ourselves. We've trained ourselves to think in "if onlys"—if only our spouse would come home from work earlier, we'd be happy; if only we'd make $20,000 more a year, we'd be happy; if only we could be a stay-at-home mom, we'd be happy. We spend our time trying to make our "if onlys" come true only to discover that even if we do achieve them, a new "if only" arises.

That was certainly true for me. For most of my first forty years, I was your average negative person. I would religiously catalog all that was wrong with my life and spend my time and energy trying to create a happier tomorrow. But when getting what I was sure would make me happy didn't—independence, money, success—I realized that I'd been looking in all the wrong places. So I decided to do a happiness makeover. This twelve-year process has led me to write a series of books on the virtues of kindness, gratitude, generosity, patience, and self-trust as ways to be happy, and to now look at happiness head-on. I've studied happy people, read all the books, done a lot of soul-searching, worked hard on myself, and offered a helping hand to my clients.

This week, I got a bit of validation that I'm getting somewhere. We've been doing work in our backyard, and I invited the contractor and his wife to dinner as a thank-you. I'd spoken maybe twenty-five words to them beforehand. We had our normal family time, including after-dinner dancing in the living room with Ana. The next day, the man came to the door to thank me. "That was nice," he said with a smile. "You're really happy, aren't you?"

I am, I thought, and it's taken fifty years of work to get here. Maybe that's why I've written this book—so that others won't have to struggle so long, so that more of us can answer a resounding yes, so that happiness can blossom to its fullness for ourselves and for those we encounter on our path.

Happiness is its own reward, but it doesn't stop there. Happy people are accepting of themselves, so they don't spend precious time in regret. They accept others, too, so are free to love people as they are, rather than expending energy trying to do a repair job on everyone in sight. They look positively to the future so they don't spend a lot of time in worry or fear. They are engaged with life as a wonderful adventure in which they are here to give their best. The zest with which they encounter life is contagious; people are drawn into their orbit and success seems to be attracted as well. They're healthier too. A study reported recently in the *Journal of Neurology* found that happy older people are less likely to develop Alzheimer's disease. Studies have also found that folks who are happy are less likely to die prematurely or even develop colds.

As I've thought, read, and practiced the art of happiness, I've come to understand a few things: first, that the search for happiness is at the root of all human activity throughout the ages; second, that happiness must be experienced in this moment or risk never being felt at all. While we can get nostalgic for the past—*oh, I used to be so happy*—or wistful about the future—*someday I will be happy*—it is now, in this very moment, that we must create the only happiness that we can count on.

Most important, I've learned that while scientists have recently discovered we each have a genetic happiness set point, a place on the emotional spectrum we tend to drift toward, it accounts for only 40–50 percent of our happiness (which they determined by studying twins raised apart). What that means is that we all can experience more contentment and joyfulness no matter who we are. For as of yet, no one has discovered an upward limit on good feelings.

In a very real sense, happiness is the ultimate makeover. Why else do we spend money and time on fixing our houses, our bodies, our relationships except that we want to be happier? Rather than trying to shore up baggy eyelids or redo mismatched furniture in an attempt to experience greater overall satisfaction and enjoyment, why not go directly to the source—cultivating the mental and emotional outlooks that will generate a sense of joyfulness independent of couch fabric or lipstick brand?

As I studied and practiced, I've come to understand that happiness is a feeling that arises as a result of thoughts we choose to hold and actions we choose to take to increase those good thoughts. In this way, we think our way to happiness.

At the heart of this book is the realization that the mind is a powerful thing and its power can be used to make us happy or miserable. We can concentrate on how the world has done us wrong or the ways it does us right. We can focus on where we're stuck or how we're free. We can take the opportunity to notice the ordinary miracles around us. We can find ways to truly enjoy, even to relish, the moments of our lives.

While certain thinking creates happiness, happiness itself may also create better thinking: "[T]here is a growing body of evidence that people think more effectively and expansively when they are happy than when they are not," noted Professor Barry Schwartz in a recent speech to Swarthmore graduates. For instance, doctors who were given bags of candy before seeing patients—a happiness booster—increased their accuracy and speed of diagnosis.

Before psychology got interested in happiness, about ten years ago, this topic was left to philosophers. Since Aristotle, philosophers have distinguished between hedonistic happiness, happiness as a feeling of pleasure or contentment, and eudaimonistic happiness, which arises out of satisfaction with one's actions and character. Recently positive psychology has made a similar distinction between pleasure and gratification, noting that since pleasure is fleeting and gratification longer lasting, it is better to pursue gratification to experience "authentic" happiness. The distinction may be intellectually useful, but I think it fails to take into account the uniqueness of each person and therefore what each of us may need.

Take me, for instance. I knew a lot about the happiness that comes from living your strengths and values (what Martin Seligman calls the path of gratification). But until recently I knew precious little about enjoying my life moment to moment, the pleasure path. What I want to encourage you to do, dear reader, is understand which of the paths to happiness you need to pursue in your own makeover and to cultivate the thinking that will lead you there.

There Are Many Paths to Happiness

"Happiness, that grand mistress of
ceremonies in the dance of life, impels us
through all its mazes and meanderings, but
leads none of us by the same route."

—*Charles Caleb Colton*

Fred, a harried marketing executive, contacted me because he wanted to be happier. We chatted about what he could do to make his life feel better, but I could tell we weren't getting anywhere. He kept focusing on his problems—an unresponsive boss, children who were struggling in school. So I asked him to make a study of the happy people he knew—what was different between them and him?—and then report back on what he observed.

Two weeks later, Fred called. "People who are happy are more appreciative," he told me. "They take action on the things they can in their lives, and don't worry about the rest. And they smile more." So Fred and I laid out a plan for him to learn to do these three things. On a daily basis, he began looking at what he could appreciate about his life—healthy children, a job, a solid marriage. Then he began taking action where he could—better training for his employees so he wouldn't have to do so much himself, setting boundaries with the kids (making it clear there were consequences for not doing assigned chores, for instance)—and letting go of the rest. Every time he found himself worrying about something he could not control, he would stop and refocus. He began to look each day for at least one "rosebush of happiness," as I call those little pleasures of everyday life that bring us enjoyment and make us smile. And what do you know? He got happier.

Another client came to me, same issue. I gave her the same assignment and she came back saying, "Happy people have more fun. They take time to play." So I helped her figure out how she could do more of that. A third person said that happy people are kinder and more generous than she. A fourth reported that happy people are passionately consumed by meaningful work.

I've given the happy people study to dozens of folks. And lo and behold, everyone discovers something different! What I've come to see is that each of us notices exactly what we need to learn—that's why we notice it. So rather than giving too much credence to what the research says or taking anyone else's word for what creates happiness, conduct a study for yourself and pay attention to what you discover. That will be the key to your own successful makeover.

This is not to say that there aren't themes in what they found. No one said other people were happier because they have more stuff or fewer problems. No one said it was because others were rich or famous. In fact, the things they and others discovered form the basis of this book. But which things you need to concentrate on most likely will be revealed in your study of happy people, as well as the ideas that resonate most strongly for you as you read along. Both are signals of the path that will yield the best results for you personally. So let your heart, mind, and spirit guide you to the practices and ideas that are just right for you.

The Happiness Makeover offers stories from my life and those I've worked with and read about, and a blend of emotional, spiritual, philosophical, and practical perspectives drawn from positive psychology, Eastern and Western wisdom traditions, and asset-focused coaching. Along the way, I try to suggest approaches that really work; at the bottom, I'm a fundamentally practical soul. I try to avoid offering pat or insipid solutions that are impossible to enact—a recent *Reader's Digest*, for instance, citing research, advised readers that one of the keys to happiness was to be married; another was to have religious faith. What effect does that have on the millions of single people searching for love or those who struggle with faith? It leaves them standing outside the candy store window, unable to partake of the goodies inside. *The Happiness Makeover* is intended to help anyone, regardless of your race, religious affiliation, income level, gender, or marital status, to experience the joy, contentment, and satisfaction that are your human birthright.

At bottom, happiness is not an idea but a feeling—of lightness, of well-being, the "relaxed at-ease state of your being with existence" as spiritual teacher Osho describes it. As you begin the journey, it helps to understand that what you are engaging in is nothing more or less than mind training, the creation of new habits of thought that in turn generate positive feelings.

A Happiness Makeover Is
Like Training a Puppy

"The happiness of your life depends upon
the quality of your thoughts, therefore
guard accordingly; and take care that
you entertain no notions unsuitable to
virtue, and reasonable nature."

—*Marcus Aurelius Antoninus*

Ana got a puppy for her seventh birthday. "I never knew it was so much work!" she exclaimed after the first week. As we struggled with the (seemingly endless) task of housebreaking little Mooky, I was struck by how similar it is to training your mind to happiness.

At first, the puppy just goes where she wants to, whenever the urge strikes. Your job as trainer is to keep putting her where you want her to go, namely outside, at the right time. Punishment doesn't work so well; it's better to keep putting her outside—no, not here, over here—and offering a lot of praise and rewards. Over time, she gets the point and it takes no effort on your part anymore. She's done it so many times correctly that it becomes automatic.

That's also the theory behind a happiness makeover. Right now, your mind is like an untrained puppy, wandering all over the place, often making you miserable. The more you become aware where your mind automatically goes and place it where you want it to go, the more you create the neurological pathway to that better choice, and the more automatic that choice becomes. And the reward is found in how good you will feel.

In a sense, unlike a puppy, your mind is already trained—to go to thoughts of worry, negativity, gloom. Your job is to retrain it. Recent breakthroughs in the ability to see the brain function—through MRIs—reveal that we all have two prefrontal lobes in our neocortex. When the left is activated, we think thoughts of peace, happiness, joy, contentment, optimism. When the right is activated, we think thoughts of gloom, doom, worry, pessimism. It turns out that each of us has what they call a tilt—a tendency for whatever happens to stimulate one side or the other. That's what creates the difference between optimists and pessimists. Whether we're born that way or develop it very young is not clear. But by the time we're adults, we have a deeply grooved tendency to activate either the right (negative) or left (positive) no matter what's going on.

An illustrative story: My friend and I were lost on a mountaintop in Utah. I began instantly worrying. How will we ever get down? What if we freeze to death up here? My friend was looking around saying things like, "Look at this fabulous scenery! Isn't it breathtaking!" Same event, but she has a left prefrontal tilt and I have a right. Therefore, in precisely the same circumstance, she is happy and I am not.

Here's the great news for anyone whose mind goes to the gloomy right. With practice you can create a left tilt. First you have to catch yourself in your negative habitual thinking. Then you have to choose to think about things in a peaceful, optimistic way. Over time, you'll be doing it without thinking about it. You do this just like training the puppy. When you find yourself going down the bad old road, you simply stop and, without beating yourself up, choose the other path. You're not trying to get rid of the old habit—it's a deeply grooved neurological path. What you're doing is building a pathway to a new habit, each time you stop and make a different choice.

Many people have gotten half of this message. With awareness, they've learned to stop when they notice themselves driving down the old negative road. *Don't go there!* they say to themselves. But our minds want to go *somewhere*—it takes a lot of energy to stop thinking. You can't just stop the negative; you have to give your mind somewhere good to go. This means practicing thinking thoughts of kindness, patience, generosity, or gratitude that may feel awkward initially. But with practice, such positive thoughts will become natural and you won't have to work so much at happiness.

In a real way, this book is about choices for thinking to activate your left prefrontal cortex as much as possible. Because that's where happiness resides.

As you enter into this training process, here are four things to keep in mind:

1. It takes practice to create the new pathway.

2. Shoulds only get in your way—one of the greatest tools for change is awareness without judgment. Just notice and choose the other option.

3. Learning is enhanced through reflection after an event (but not by beating yourself up).

4. Once you've created the new habit, it will be yours for life!

This approach of focusing on the positive is not a plea to ignore or deny the challenges, sorrows, and grief in our lives. They are real. And it doesn't mean that we feel fabulous all the livelong day. But the possibility of experiencing the joy of being alive, of appreciating what we can in our circumstances, of letting go of unnecessary burdens, of giving to others—is also real. We have what we need to be happy. In every moment, we can choose where to focus our attention and therefore how we feel. The difficulties of our lives get a lot of our mental airtime and sap a great deal of our life force. How about giving equal time to happiness?

II

WHAT'S STANDING IN YOUR WAY?

"The 'decision to be happy' is actually
the decision to stop being unhappy."

—*Barry Neil Kaufman*

Each of us has particular mental habits that keep us from experiencing the maximum happiness we could feel at any given moment. Ch'an Buddhists call these "habit energies." These are our unique ways of interfering with the natural ability we all possess to experience both the exhilaration and contentment that we call happiness. In this section, we examine how you might be blocking the joy available to you in your daily life, and I offer suggestions as to how to work with some of the most common interferences, including discontent, worry, regret, envy, disappointment, grudges, perfectionism, and conflict. By working with what's standing in our way, we clear the road to discover the happiness hidden in our ordinary days.

1

Kena Hura,
Poo, Poo, Poo

What's Your Happiness Myth?

"Don't believe everything you think."
—*Bumper sticker*

"I'm afraid to say I'm happy," confessed Debra the other day. "Or at least I think I should say after it, in the words of my bubbe, 'Kena hura, poo, poo, poo.'"

"What's that?" I asked.

"It's a way of keeping the bad spirits away," she explained, "to ensure nothing ruins the existing happiness and that your current fortune continues. But it also has a sense of foreboding or superstition to it, as in 'Don't say you're happy out loud—you'll give yourself a kena hura.'"

That was a new one on me, but I recognize the sentiment. Each of us has particular family, religious, or societal traditions that teach us we're not supposed to be happy or at least not acknowledge our happiness or something bad will happen. As if there is an evil being in the sky waiting to strike us down if it notices we are happy: I'm good, knock on wood, we say. And then we knock to keep the evil away.

What's your happiness myth as passed down by your clan, church, or culture? That happiness on earth doesn't exist? That people and life are just out to screw you, so you can never let your guard down? That if you ever feel happy, it will be snatched away? Were you taught to knock on wood? That only the "right" college or career would bring happiness?

Mine is straight out of Catholicism: Life is suffering and the more you suffer in silence, the better God likes it and the better chance you have to get into heaven, which is the only place lasting happiness is to be found. We used to have a steak dinner whenever anyone in our family died to celebrate that they were no longer suffering but were happy in heaven. (I once gave a talk on happiness at Old St. Patrick's Cathedral in Chicago and a wry gentleman with an Irish brogue and his tongue firmly in his cheek commented after my talk, "I see the Dalai Lama has written a book called *The Art of Happiness*. We Irish Catholics have been writing the book of suffering for centuries.") As a consequence of this training, I was very good at deferring happiness, although I had a bit more trouble with the suffering-in-silence part.

My husband Don's myth is more personal. His father was afflicted with brain tumors in his late forties, just as he was on the verge of buying the car and house of his dreams. Don's myth is if you get close to what will make you happy, you'll die. So he makes sure he always stays slightly discontent and unsure about what will bring him happiness.

A writer I know learned from her family that creative people are always tortured. So while she has found tremendous success and acclaim from her writing, she can't allow herself to enjoy either the success or the process itself. In order for her writing to be good, she believes, she must be miserable.

Bringing these myths into the light can be liberating. Otherwise, without our knowing it, they may be keeping us from experiencing the joyfulness and pleasure our lives can offer. Enjoying and appreciating our lives does not make bad things happen. In fact, there is some indication from the new physics that it's actually the opposite: You draw to you whatever you spend time thinking about.

My first awareness of the happiness that comes from letting go of old superstitions arose in therapy in my twenties, when I was talking about trying to find a "real" career. "Yes, I'm an editor," I said dismissively, "but it comes so easily to me. I need to find something challenging to do."

The therapist looked at me and replied, "Just because it's easy doesn't mean you shouldn't do it."

I was dumbstruck—could I really choose a path of ease and actually enjoy my work rather than using difficulty as my measure? And could I be happy here and now rather than waiting until death?

What is the myth that is holding you back from feeling the maximum happiness right in this moment? Give it a title: I Can't Get No Satisfaction; Everyone but Me Can Be Happy; Screw Them Over Before They Do It to You. Is it serving you well? Or would you rather revise it in the light of adulthood so your capacity for satisfaction and fulfillment will increase?

2

Is Your Brain Wired to See Danger Everywhere?

"Most people would rather be certain they're miserable, than risk being happy."
—*Robert Anthony*

Sam had a terrible childhood, with a physically abusive father and emotionally absent mother. His early years were a battlefield. At eighteen, he finally escaped with his life. Sam is now forty, married, and hasn't communicated with his parents in years. But he has a problem—while he escaped the war zone, he's still fighting as if his very survival is at stake. He sees abusers everywhere—at work, at home, in the movies. Just making it through the day is a constant struggle.

Recent breakthroughs in brain science help shed light on why Sam, like so many of us, carries his misery with him even as circumstances change for the better. Early in life, our emotional brain—the limbic system consisting of the amygdala and the brain stem—lays down the tracks of what constitutes danger and then is constantly scanning the environment for anything that might bring us harm. When harm is perceived, the body/mind goes into the state of hormonal emergency known as fight or flight, readying us to take actions for our very survival.

The problem is that the emotional brain is left over from our reptilian past and therefore is not very smart. It generalizes in an attempt to make us safe, which is fine if you are a lizard looking for movement in the grasses that might indicate a predator. But in complex human situations, the on and off switch can be too generalized, so that we end up seeing danger in every corner and can have the fight or flight switch on almost all the time, flooding our bodies with stress hormones such as adrenaline and cortisol.

That's what's going on with Sam. His emotional brain sees danger everywhere in an attempt to keep him safe. Unfortunately, it is making him miserable. Does he want to be miserable? Not really. In fact, he's come to work with me because he wants to stop being so unhappy. But he's afraid. He's afraid that if he lets down his guard and experiences happiness, some terrible thing will sneak up on him while he's not paying attention.

Sam is not alone. Many of us feel exactly the same way. I for one have found much liberation in understanding that it's not personal. It's not because I want to be unhappy and fearful. It's the way our brains are structured.

The good news has to do with brain structure also: we also have thinking brains, made up primarily of the neocortex. When we find ourselves going into fear, we can ask ourselves, *Am I really in danger? What's the best way to respond to this situation?* That puts our thinking brain into gear. From that place, we can evaluate whether we need to run or fight or are just being tricked by our amygdala. It doesn't always work. Neuroscientists have discovered that the limbic system has a pathway that allows it to escape control of the cortex when it gets worked up enough about something. It's called an amygdala hijack.

However, the more we practice engaging our thinking brain at highly charged emotional moments, the more freedom of choice we have. That's what Sam learned to do. He practiced letting his guard down by questioning his automatic fear response and getting his neocortex going. And he learned that if his amygdala did get the best of him, it takes at least thirty minutes for the stress hormones to begin to dissipate. So he removed himself from others until he could be reasonable again.

The capacity for the neocortex to override our feeling brain is why we can, to a great extent, think ourselves happier. It doesn't always work, but the more we understand that much of our unhappiness comes from old fear, the more we free ourselves to experience greater contentment and joy today.

3

Do You Motivate Yourself Through Discontent?

"You create problems so that you can
feel that life is a great work, a growth,
and you have to struggle hard."

—*Osho*

When Don and I first started living together, it was so easy that I thought something was seriously wrong. I was used to relationships that were full of drama and struggle, where we "worked" on issues (not that the work got us anywhere, but we felt like we were trying), and I spent all of my mental energy on trying to fix the other person. What was I supposed to do all day, I asked my friend Daphne, if not work on or worry about my relationship? "Enjoy the peacefulness," she advised, "and if you need something to fill the time, take up knitting."

I never did learn to knit, but I have learned to be happy and content in love. And I can tell you it sure felt awkward at first.

I don't think I'm alone. I believe that lots of us don't experience the happiness available to us because we use our unhappiness to motivate ourselves. The fact that there's always a problem to be fixed keeps us going. Perhaps it comes from the Protestant work ethic that still permeates this culture, but many of us unconsciously suspect that if we're happy, we'll sit around and accomplish nothing. So we make sure there's always a problem. If it isn't love that has our knickers in a twist, it's work. Or our parents or children.

This discontent is also fueled by the attention—of the media, the educational system, psychology, our families—on what's wrong with us rather than what's right. Rather than celebrating our strengths and gifts, we tend to focus on all our foibles and failings—and those around us—and therefore view life as a selfimprovement project.

What if we changed our orientation? What would happen if we saw our life as something to be savored, rather than as a series of problems to be solved? Here's how a friend, a working mother with two small kids, put it in a recent e-mail: "I'm embracing the fact that there will never be enough time for work, for children, for marriage, for me... for about 15 years. It's just a fact of life, so I try to really enjoy all the moments—and there are many precious, wonderful moments these days."

When we are motivated by happiness, it doesn't mean that we ignore our difficulties. Rather, like my friend said, we embrace our lives wholeheartedly, the good and the not so good, and relax into it, not making the bad worse by denial or drama. Is my relationship with Don perfect? Of course not. I could give you a laundry list of all his faults and my faults and the imperfections of our marriage. But I've learned the hard way that a relationship is not a fix-it project; what's needed is much more acceptance of the way it is and enjoyment of what is wonderful rather than an attempt to fix every flaw. And when issues begin to truly get in our way, we do deal with them.

When we motivate ourselves through happiness, life gets easier. It flows. We're not so busy fighting reality, but instead spend our time enjoying what we can about the way it is. Recently I was talking to a young friend who got married a while ago. She was having in-law problems. Her husband's family had a looser sense of planning than she, and she was constantly frustrated by their impromptu behavior. "I doubt you are going to change this entire family system," I commented. "But you could spend a lot of your life trying. Will that make you happy?"

"No," she replied. "If I want to be happy, the best thing to do would be to volunteer to be the planner and then not get so caught up in their following my plans to the letter."

Has being discontented gotten you what you want in your life? At what price? What if you rested in the easy, wonderful aspects of your life rather than trying to fix what was broken? What would happen if you tried, even for a week, to motivate yourself by asking, *What would really bring me happiness now?*

4

What's So Bad about Getting Your Hopes Up?

"Pessimist: One who, when he has the choice of two evils, chooses both."

—Oscar Wilde

There was a reorganization at Don's work, and it looked like he was going to get to do more of what he was good at. But he was moping around. "This is great," I said. "Why aren't you celebrating?"

"Well," he replied, "I don't know for sure, so I don't want to get my hopes up."

Don's not alone—I know dozens of people who would rather keep themselves back from happiness now in case the situation turns out to be not what they wanted. I used to be one of them. From a very young age, to avoid disappointment I made sure that I didn't get my hopes up, no matter what. As a consequence, I spent most of my life in the gray tepid zone, dipping down from there to misery, but never indulging in opportunities for the bright colors of hope or exhilaration.

What's that about anyway? Why not, if the occasion warrants it, rejoice today? Life presents many challenges and difficulties, so why miss out on any opportunity to feel exceptionally good? Take Don, for instance. Why would it be bad for him to celebrate today the possibility of his new position? He would feel great today. Then tomorrow, when he goes into work and finds out more, he would either feel even better or he would feel worse. But his happiness today will not influence the outcome, and I don't believe he would feel worse at having rejoiced than if he hadn't.

Behind this attitude is a belief that if you don't experience happiness, you won't have to experience disappointment. Of course you will—whenever you don't get what you want, you're likely to experience a sense of loss. That's natural. Not being happy at potential good fortune in case it doesn't work out is like not risking falling in love because someday it might end—you may stay "safe," but you cut yourself off from many occasions for joy.

At the base, I think this "don't get your hopes up" is a form of magical thinking. We believe that if we get happy about something, we'll jinx it. I remember clearly when I first started my publishing company and we were auctioning off the paperback rights to our first book. We had two big publishers competing; as they went back and forth, the amount of money got higher and higher. The day ended without a conclusion—they would continue to bid the next day. At that moment, our share would be big enough to fund the press for a year. But rather than being excited, I was terrified: What if something went wrong? I could not sleep for worrying about getting my hopes dashed. Why was it so hard to feel happy? My happiness was not going to make the money melt away. And if the deal did fall through, at least I would have had a wonderful evening rather than biting my nails over the possibility of something bad happening!

I didn't change my ways overnight. But when I saw how much time I spent holding myself back for no good reason, I began to allow myself a bit of excitement, happiness even, when good fortune came my way, even when it wasn't guaranteed (for of course there really are no guarantees anyway). And the more I did, I found many more occasions to be happy on a daily basis and, so far, have been able to withstand the dashing of my hopes when sometimes that occurs.

This happiness hindrance is so common. Just as I was wondering how to finish this essay, my phone rang. It was a friend who had been house hunting for six months. She'd just made an offer and it had been accepted. She was thrilled. "But my realtor said not to get too excited until the signed contract was in hand," she explained.

"Why not?" I replied. "You get as excited as you want."

"I will," she exclaimed as she hung up the phone, "and I'm starting right now!"

5

Are You Envious of Others?

"One always thinks others are happy."

—*Yiddish saying*

Rachel was turning thirty-five. As is common with decade and half-decade birthdays, it was a time when her whole life came up for examination. Yes, she thought, I do have a husband and a baby and a job. But look at Lana, who's my exact age. Her career is much more successful than mine—she's well known in her field and makes scads of money. "I felt like a failure, like I hadn't accomplished as much in my life as I should have by now," she explained to me one day. "Then my husband threw me a big party and Lana came. We got to talking about our lives and she said to me, 'You know, I really envy you your husband and baby. I'm not getting any younger and sometimes I despair of ever finding lasting love and having a child.'

"That's when I really got it," exclaimed Rachel, "we're all going around assuming others are better off than we are and feeling miserable in comparison rather than enjoying what we do have. It was a wake-up call—I stopped wishing to be her and started being happy with who I am and what I have."

Rachel's experience is not uncommon. Rather than being content with what we've got, the comparing mind is always sizing up our situation against others and finding our lives lacking, destroying the happiness we could be experiencing. What I've learned is that it's useless to tell ourselves not to do it—it's part of the function of the brain to compare.

There are only two ways I know to deal with comparisons. The first is to be conscious of whom we are comparing ourselves to. A friend of mine makes $100,000 a year. She's constantly comparing herself to famous people making millions. I often remind her that she is in the upper 5 percent of women wage earners in the United States and so, compared to the vast majority of people in the world, she makes a great deal of money. One comparison makes her happier, the other miserable.

Scientists call looking at those less fortunate downward comparison, and it is remarkably effective at boosting our happiness. For instance, a study was done in which some folks were asked to complete this sentence five times: "I'm glad I'm not a..." Others were asked to complete this one: "I wish I were a..." Both were asked how satisfied they were with their lives before and after. Guess what? Those in the "I'm glad" group's happiness rating went up significantly after the exercise, while those in the other's went down markedly.

This approach to happiness used to make me a bit queasy. It felt wrong to me to boost myself up on the back of others' suffering. But studies now show that people who do are actually *more* likely to help others, to volunteer or work toward alleviating social injustice because of their awareness of their blessings.

Another way to deal with comparison is the one Rachel stumbled upon—to begin to tell one another the truth about our lives. We tend not to share the difficulties with our lives with others, saying "great" or "fine" when someone asks us how we are doing. But, as Dennis Prager notes in *Happiness Is a Serious Problem,* "we pay a price for everyone's putting on a happy face—we start believing that life for everyone else is great." Everyone struggles with inner demons, everyone has challenges. The more we share them with one another, the less alone we feel and the more we understand every life is a mix of happiness and sadness. In a real sense, intimacy is the antidote to comparison envy.

That's the reason, I think, why shows like Dr. Phil's and Dr. Laura's are so popular—we experience others with all their warts showing and recognize that no one has it all together. The same is true for gossip magazines. We get to prove to ourselves that stars, despite fame and fortune, are no happier than we are. They struggle with addictions, have trouble with children, have bad hair days, can't find lasting love.

So the next time you find yourself feeling unhappy in comparison to the wonderfulness of someone else's life, think about those less fortunate than you. And find out more about the supposed happiness paragon's disappointments and sorrows. Chances are, like Rachel, you'll find out that he or she is envying you for something too! And then use that conversation as a reminder to enjoy the wonders of your own life.

6

Is Your Head Full of Negative Self-Talk?

The mind is its own place,
And in itself can make
A Heav'n of Hell,
Or a Hell of Heav'n.

—*John Milton*

Like many of us, Cynthia's head is full of shame and blame and guilt. Needless to say, she's unhappy a lot—she's got an internal torture chamber going most of the time. She's done a lot of therapy and meditation. As a consequence, she's become very aware of this inner voice. However, she's still stuck, she recently told me, because "I've not been too willing to counteract it. Mostly I just notice it, and then let it carry me away."

Cynthia is on to something very important when it comes to working with happiness hindrances. Awareness of negative thinking, while it is crucial for change—you have to recognize what you are doing that you want to do differently—may not be enough. In fact, like Cynthia, it may make you feel worse as you become aware of just how much you do it. Rather, you need to begin to counteract the negative thoughts so that they begin to loosen their grip.

In his work on learned optimism, Martin Seligman notes that we need to treat negative thoughts "as if they were uttered by an external person whose mission is to make your life miserable," he explains in *Authentic Happiness,* "and then [marshal] evidence against the thoughts." Clients I've worked with find it helpful to give this person a name; it creates a distance between you and the negative thinking so that it controls you less. You can even learn to joke about it—"Oh yeah, there you are again trying to drive me crazy."

Oftentimes the voices are those of early caretakers who taught us to treat ourselves this way. Now we're grown, but they're still in our heads ranting on. They've had years of airtime—isn't it about time to free yourself by talking back?

If you hear yourself think, "I can't do anything right," stop and recall three things you've done right. If you think, "I should be able to do this; I'm such a loser," stop and think, "I may have made a mistake this time, but I can learn." Because we're often hardest on ourselves, it may help to ask, *If this were a friend or loved one who had done this, how would I respond to them?* Then say or write that to yourself. If you get stuck and can't think of any positive thought to substitute, ask a kind friend how he or she would respond.

If this is truly challenging for you, cognitive therapy, which teaches how to change your thinking to change your feelings, might be useful. Or check out *The Feeling Good Handbook* by David D. Burns, M.D.

Such negative self-talk is not natural. Once the Dalai Lama was speaking with Western psychologists who were asking him about the problem of low self-esteem in American meditators. He looked puzzled—he didn't know what they were talking about. The concept was completely foreign to him. Over and over, they explained it in different ways—chronic self-criticism, negative self-regard. Finally he understood. "This is not a good thing," he said simply.

It's *not* a good thing. Each and every one of us deserves to live in peace, both external and internal. The more we learn to counteract the negativity in our minds, the more happiness will find room to bloom in our hearts.

7

Are You Caught in the Never-Ending Desire for More Stuff?

"Even if all our dreams came true, it
would never be enough. The nature
of desire is to constantly crave."
—*Howard Raphael Cushnir*

My friend Heather is thirtysomething, newly married, and thinking of kids. She went to a department store recently and noticed that many of the TV characters she loved as a child are now back: Strawberry Shortcake and Scooby-Doo adorn every conceivable children's product: lunch boxes, pillows, clothes. "How cute. What goes around, comes around," she surmised. Then she saw a marketing documentary and discovered that it was no coincidence. "They are trying to get me to buy that stuff by reminding me of my childhood," she declared as she stormed into my house.

Welcome to the wonderful world of consumer society, in which the engine of the economy is fueled by extremely sophisticated, segmented-by-age-race-gender-and-who-knows-what-else attempts to get us to purchase things we don't need by playing on feelings of nostalgia (you can go back to those good old days when you were happy) or lack (you won't feel happy unless you have this thing).

The traps of nostalgia and lack work so well because they are naturally occurring human phenomena: It is a basic tendency of people to be dissatisfied, to long for the good old days or to believe that some different, other thing will finally make them happy. The only thing that's different these days is that the array of possible products has grown exponentially and contemporary marketing has gotten incredibly skilled at exploiting those tendencies. So our sense of dissatisfaction has grown to become a ravenous beast threatening not only to bankrupt us individually but to bury the world in a morass of stuff.

What this avalanche of products and "carefully crafted campaigns of planned obsolescence" has done, says philosopher Mark Kingwell, is to create "Upgrade Angst," an "energy-sapping anxiety" that we are somehow being left behind if we don't consume all the products possible to us in every given moment.

No wonder we're not happy! We are bombarded daily by messages precisely designed to make us feel miserable so that we will consume more. But consuming more fails to make us happy and so we become even more vulnerable to the very ad campaigns that sucked us into the morass to begin with, as we are told that this next thing will finally offer the cure. Philip Saltier articulated the problem like this: "Americans become unhappy... because their preoccupation with amassing possessions obliterates their loneliness. This is why production in America seems to be on such an endless upward spiral: every time we buy something we deepen our emotional deprivation and hence our need to buy something."

So what's a person to do? The answer, I believe, is to see behind the curtain, to recognize the smoke and mirrors, as did Dorothy and her friends in *The Wizard of Oz*. There is no magic happiness lying in wait in the newest car, computer, or Manolo Blahnik shoes. Craving—*I have to have!*—is a fundamental aspect of human existence. That's what the Buddha meant by the First Noble Truth.

Once we really understand that wanting stuff is just something minds do, we begin to have a choice: to fall into the trap over and over, or to relate to it, talk back to it. Oh there you are, you craving. You're trying to fool me into thinking I'll be happy if only I buy this $100 skirt. I may experience a flutter of pleasure, but how am I going to feel when the credit card bill comes in? What could I do instead right now that would bring me some lasting happiness—call a friend, finish that project, volunteer at the homeless shelter like I've been talking about forever?

I'm not saying that we should never purchase things—my house is full of them. But we can do so with greater consciousness, so that we always remember that real happiness is found in places other than the mall.

8

Do You Need to Give Up Grudges?

"When we hate our enemies, we are giving them power over us: power over our sleep, our appetites, our blood pressure, our health, and our happiness. Our enemies would dance with joy if only they knew how they were worrying us, lacerating us, and getting even with us! Our hate is not hurting them at all, but our hate is turning our own days and nights into a hellish turmoil."

—*Dale Carnegie*

When my fourteen-year relationship ended, it was not of my choosing. I was heartbroken, devastated, angry. My whole world threatened to tumble down around me. Will and I not only lived together, but were the co-owners of Conari Press, a small independent book publisher.

In all of my pain and anger, one thing was clear: I did not want to lose my company as well as my spouse. For about the first six months, he made himself scarce, which allowed me to find my footing again. But one day he arrived back at the office, planning to work full-time. Neither of us could afford to buy the other out. I had to find a way to work with him for the good of the company—and for my own happiness. We ended up working together for ten more years, until we jointly decided to sell.

People always asked me how I did it. Mostly I did it by thinking of Conari as our child; I didn't want to destroy my child with bitterness or recrimination. It wasn't always easy, my heart hurt for years, but by remembering what really mattered to me, I was able to put the hurt aside and move on.

None of us gets through life without experiencing the slings and arrows of hurts imposed, intentionally or not, by others. We may be wounded through neglect, emotional, physical, or sexual abuse, carelessness, cynicism, abandonment—the list of ways human beings harm one another is abysmally long. These wounds are real and our pain is also. We need our pain seen, felt, heard, and our wounds dressed. This takes time, attention, compassion— and often professional help.

At some point in our healing, however, if we want to be happy, we also need to forgive. Otherwise, we pile on our backs the weight of past injuries and sorrows until the burden gets so heavy that we become immobilized by grudges.

Another word for it is embittered. It's impossible to be bitter and happy; bitterness is about taking a perverse delight in stroking our wounds, becoming so wrapped up in them that they become the way we know ourselves. From this place, we want to inflict as much suffering as we can on those we believe have harmed us, doing harm to ourselves in the process. I know a woman in the midst of an angry divorce who went against the advice of her own lawyer and refused to take a reasonable settlement because she "wanted to screw the bastard." Guess who got hurt? She and her four children, as the judge ended up awarding her less than what the ex had offered.

Much has been written in the past decade about forgiveness, saying that we really do it not for the other person, but for ourselves so that we can move on. And I believe that's true. But the best thing I've ever read about this challenging act was in psychotherapists Robert A. Johnson's and Jerry M. Ruhl's book *Contentment:* "We have utilized numerous psychological tools to try to facilitate [forgiveness], but in the end it seems that most people are not willing to let go until they have something more important to move on to."

That feels true to me. We must want something more than our grudge in order to be willing to let it go. Whether it's forgiving an ex-spouse, your parents, a boss, a random stranger, to let go we need something to move on to—another relationship, a new job, a different dream. Whatever that moving on is specifically, ultimately it's a decision to be happier. The head of New Skete monastery, Father Laurence, explained it to his community like this: "The beginning of forgiveness is a conscious act of will, not a feeling. But it also carries with it the resolve to work on changing our thoughts and dealing with our feelings."

One way to begin is to realize you have a choice, a choice to be stuck and unhappy, which you're making every day as long as you hold on to your resentment, or to let go even if it's hard to do. To start, ask yourself: *Would I rather hold this grudge or be happy? Would I rather withhold forgiveness or be happy?* If the answer is you'd rather be happy, seek out the help—therapy, spiritual counseling—you need to make the choice to move on.

9

Do You Expect Life to Be Fair?

"If all our happiness is bound up entirely in our personal circumstances it is difficult not to demand of life more than it has to give."
—*Bertrand Russell*

Four people began a business that required a tremendous amount of sweat equity. They worked sixty- to eighty-hour weeks for about a year without pay. Just as they were getting to the breakeven point, one of them made an announcement: She was pregnant and was going to take maternity leave of three months after the baby was born. And she needed to cut back her hours now because her obstetrician had advised her to.

That's when I got called in. The trio left behind was angry. "It's not fair!" they said. And continued to say for months. All they could focus on was the injustice of it all. They were paying me to speak my mind, and so I eventually did. I told them that they had a right to feel upset. They were being put in a hard position. But focusing on how unfair it was wasn't going to solve their problem. It might not be fair, but it was reality. Their joint task was to figure out how to respond most effectively given what they all cared about—the success of their business. Given the current reality, how best should they move forward?

Life is not fair. Just ask anyone who gets seriously ill or injured through no fault of their own. Or those who lose their house to an earthquake, tornado, or other "act of God." Or a job to outsourcing. All manner of difficult, painful, or tragic things happen due to circumstances beyond our control. If we base our happiness on the fairness of life, we are absolutely doomed to misery. Very few of us get through the length of a lifetime without having our share of random events knock us upside the head. Dealing with the pain and upheaval such events create is hard enough without creating the added expectation that life should not treat us this way.

When such things happen, it's not personal. The world is not out to screw us over. We just happen to be in the path of the oncoming car. All we can really do is treat ourselves kindly as we take stock of the damage and figure out how to move forward as happily as possible under the circumstances. When we expect or demand that life be fair, we impede the process toward resolution and/or healing and therefore get stuck.

That's where my entrepreneurs were. Here was a situation they could not control. It was better, therefore, to use their energy to find the best solution to what was rather than lamenting over how it should be. Eventually, they did find their way through. The three worked more hours, and the woman gave up some of her equity to compensate them for their efforts.

Recently, I heard the newest chapter in the story. It turns out the trio was happier running the business without the new mom, and she was happier staying home. So they've parted ways, happier all around.

Are you missing a chance for happiness right now by clinging to the belief that life must be fair? How might you look at the situation in a way that increases your freedom and happiness? Even though it doesn't feel good, could you see it as a learning opportunity? A way to grow your patience, your empathy, your compassion toward others?

Life isn't fair, but it sure is full of opportunities for growing our adaptability, resilience, and self-reliance. And for cultivating an inner, unshakable core to see us through hard times. That stability alone is happiness in my book!

10

Is Worry a
Constant Companion?

"First ask yourself: What is the worst thing
that could happen? Then prepare to accept
it. Then proceed to improve on the worst."

—*Dale Carnegie*

Renee was having difficulties at work and worried she was
going to be fired. When she poured out her troubles to a
friend, the friend asked her whether that was the worst
thing that could happen to her. "Of course not," she replied,
"that would be something happening to my husband."
In fact, upon reflection, she realized that losing her job
wouldn't even make it into her top ten worst things. Armed
with that perspective, she returned to work in a happier
frame of mind. And from that place, she worked through
the conflict with her boss, and the crisis was soon over.

If you're stuck in worry a lot, it often works, as Dale
Carnegie points out in the above quote, to think of the
worst first and get it out of the way. That's what Renee did.
Luckily for her, what she discovered was that it didn't matter as much to her as she thought originally. That realization gave her the resilience and buoyancy to see the matter
through to a good conclusion.

But what if it is something in your top ten? How do you keep your spirits up? Looking at the worst-case scenario can actually help because it allows you to get out of your emotional brain, where worry may be swamping you, and move over to your thinking brain, where you can work through all that could possibly go wrong in order to plan for every contingency. Just the planning itself can provide relief. So can the realization that most everything is survivable.

For instance, Kathi had to have a lumpectomy to determine if she had breast cancer. Her mother and sister had both had it, so it was realistic to consider that she might also. Immediately she went into planning mode about what she would do if it were cancer—whether to take a leave of absence, what doctor she would want, what support she could count on. She felt better knowing that she could cope.

Once you've planned for the worst, then it's time to hope for the best. This is the part I used to have a lot of trouble with. I used to believe that if I focused all my energy on what could go wrong, it would somehow prevent it from happening. So after my risk analysis, I would make myself miserable by concentrating on all the possible terrible outcomes. Experience finally taught me that all that did was make me miserable as I waited for the results and that most of the terrible things I anticipated never came about anyway. So I decided that I would hope for the best—at least I would be happier while waiting!

That's what Kathi did, too. She decided to be as happy as she could be while waiting for the test and the results, to enjoy her health as much as possible. And when the test came back negative, she was very glad she had chosen to be hopeful during those several weeks.

If you tend toward worry, think the worst first—then plan to create the best outcome.

11

Do Expectations Get in Your Way?

"Blessed is he who expects nothing,
for he shall never be disappointed."
—*Alexander Pope*

A friend was complaining about her mother. "I hate all the holidays—Christmas, Thanksgiving, Easter, birthdays, Mother's Day, anniversaries. No matter what we do or what we give her, my mom's never happy. It's as though she has an idea or image in her head of the perfect day and we can never match that image no matter what we do."

This woman's mother suffers from too many expectations—the desire, often below our level of awareness and therefore unarticulated, that other people must behave in a particular way or else we'll be unhappy. As a consequence, this woman is always disappointed. Even if she became aware of her expectations and stated them to her family, chances are she would still be unhappy. That's because expectations are one of the greatest happiness killers there is. They create bitterness when you didn't get what you expected and don't allow you to enjoy the surprise of whatever you did receive.

Ironically, expectations kill happiness whether you get what you want or not. Let's say you expect someone to hire you for a particular job. If she or he doesn't, you suffer great disappointment. If they do, you take it for granted because you assumed they were going to. Therefore, you don't experience happiness because you don't feel gratitude, which is the feeling of happiness when we are aware we've received something.

When it comes to the behavior of others, whether it's the person interviewing us for a job or what our relatives will do for us on Christmas, there's very little we can truly expect. We can request, we can, in the case of our children, demand. But we can't expect anything—there are just too many factors at play that have nothing to do with us. That's where gratitude comes in. When we do get what we want from others, because we know we're not in control, we don't take for granted that they responded to us in just the way we wanted. Therefore, our hearts feel full.

So if expectations get in the way of happiness, how do we approach what we want in our lives? Rather than expect things from others, I think what we're called on to do is to aspire to our own goals and dreams. Aspiration is inner directed, it comes from our deepest core. With aspiration, rather than being dependent on anyone else's behavior, we say, *I'm going for what I want with all my being, I hope it comes to pass. Since I'm not in charge of the world, there could be all kinds of reasons beyond my control why what I want can't happen. But I will give it my all.* Rather than expecting others to fulfill our holiday dreams, for instance, we think: *I'll have a happy holiday because I'll create one no matter what anyone else does.*

With aspiration, when we get our heart's desire, we experience the happiness of achieving or receiving something we wanted. And if we don't, at least we know we've given it our all.

Here's how Oprah described aspiration in a recent article in *O*. She was writing about the moment that she decided to move to Chicago and go up against Phil Donahue. Her boss was trying to talk her out of it. She finally said to him, "You're right, I may not make it and I may be walking into unforeseen land mines. But if they don't kill me, I'll keep growing." Because she aspired to success, she now lives, she writes, "in a state of exhilarated contentment (my definition of happiness), fueled by a passion for everything I'm committed to: my show, this magazine, the people I work with, my home, my gratitude for every breath breathed in freedom and peace."

If you find yourself caught in a constant dance of expectation and disappointment, first get clear that you can't necessarily make other people behave the way you want. Then put your attention on what you truly aspire to in your life, for your own efforts are totally within your control. And then take the opportunity to give thanks for all the good things that come your way, even when they are unexpected.

12

Are You Focused on the Closed Door?

"When one door of happiness closes, another one opens, but often we look so long at the closed door that we do not see the one that has been opened to us."

—*Helen Keller*

I once knew a guy who was a successful journalist. But he longed to write fiction and ended up spending ten years on a novel that he could never finish. Rather than understanding his forte lay in other kinds of writing, he saw only his failure as a novelist. Needless to say, he was extremely unhappy.

A friend opened a workout place in a very saturated market—there are six or seven competing places within driving distance. While she's done everything right in terms of promotions, incentives, and so forth, she just doesn't have enough members to make it financially. She's unhappy too.

For any of us, it's easy to get caught up in what we can't have, especially when it comes to our dreams. It's extremely disheartening to pour our heart and soul into something only to hit a brick wall. But one of the secrets to happiness is to recognize, as Mitch Albom writes in *The Five People You Meet in Heaven,* that "all endings are also beginnings. We just don't know it at the time." When we understand that, we can stop spending so much time agonizing over the closed door and start investigating where the new door might be opening.

This doesn't mean that it's not appropriate to mourn our fate. But rather than getting stuck there, at some point we need to ask, *What does this closed door mean? Do I need simply to persevere? Or try a new approach? Or does it mean that it is time for me to look for something new?*

Very few people's lives travel a straight line from a particular dream to its fulfillment. Life is always throwing us curveballs that we must learn to respond to with grace and grit. Indeed, it is in the curves themselves that we often find the open door. The musician Julio Iglesias, for instance, wanted to be a professional athlete. He took up the guitar only after he was temporarily paralyzed while playing soccer. The artist James Whistler took up painting as a treatment for depression after he flunked out of West Point and had to give up his dream of becoming a soldier. Framing our experience in terms of open and closed doors helps us not feel like failures and asks us to engage passionately with what life is calling us to do next.

No one exemplifies the power of searching for the open door better than Helen Keller. She could have spent her life bemoaning the fact that she was blind, deaf, and mute. Instead, she attended Radcliffe College, lectured on her life with the help of companions such as Anne Sullivan interpreting, and did fund-raising and consciousness raising on the plight of blind people throughout the world. When people tired of her lectures, she developed a lighthearted vaudeville show of her life, which was enormously successful. In midlife, her house burned down, and the book she had been working on for years was destroyed. She rewrote it.

In a way, happiness can be defined as the wholehearted willingness to seek and find the open door, again and again, as our lives unfold. The unhappy novelist discovered that for himself when a friend offered him a chance to work on a troubled Hollywood script. It turns out he's good at fixing other people's stories and now makes a living as a script doctor. "All that work on my novel prepared me for what I do now," he confided to me. "Thankfully, I finally stopped obsessing about what I couldn't do and found something I love that I could."

Is life asking you to stop banging your head on the closed door and look for an open one right now?

13

Do You Suffer from Regret?

"The greatest griefs are those
we cause ourselves."
—*Sophocles*

I'm not sure I totally agree with Sophocles, but I certainly believe our greatest *preventable* griefs are the ones we cause ourselves. Particularly regret and second-guessing over choices we make. Boy, is that a recipe for misery!

I realized this the other day, when I got a cash windfall. My husband needs a new car. His is ten years old, has 150,000 miles on it, and is starting to need a lot of repairs. So we entered into discussions: Should we use the money as a down payment on a new car? Or should we put the money in the bank for our retirement and limp along with the old car? There are pros and cons to each, but as I found myself increasingly frustrated, I realized it was because I wanted both and was angry that I could not figure out how to get all of what I wanted.

Then I read a book *The Paradox of Choice* by Barry Schwartz. He points out that every decision is not only a choice for something, but a choice against something else. In other words, a trade-off. Economists label it an "opportunity cost": the price of passing up the benefits of the choice we don't take. Every single decision we make has these costs associated with them. Going to Hawaii for a vacation—surf, sand, relaxation—means living without the benefits of going to New York City instead—great food, cultural stimulation. Staying late means finishing your work, but not seeing your kids before bedtime. And unless we understand that every choice comes with a price, we will be miserable with any decision we make when we finally see the price we've had to pay.

Schwartz also points out that as the number of options increases—which it has in everything from health insurance to toothpaste—we actually end up feeling worse about *whatever* we choose. "As the number of choices go up," he explains, "the amount of time and effort that goes into any decision goes up, our expectation of how good the results will be goes up, and the likelihood that we'll feel regret about the choices we've passed up to make our choice goes up." It's an unexpected effect of greater choice, he says, that we end up making good choices objectively but feeling worse subjectively. In fact, I believe this is at the heart of why folks in affluent societies often rank low on happiness—we are less happy with our decisions because we have so many options to choose from.

What's a person who wants to be happy to do? First, Schwartz recommends, don't look to make the perfect choice, just a good enough one. Pam learned this lesson when picking an adoption agency. She spent months searching for the "right" one, only to realize after six months that reputable services are pretty much all the same. Now when prospective adoptive parents call her for advice, she suggests that they get a few recommendations, but not get hung up on the choice.

Second, understand opportunity costs. I ended up not buying a car or saving my windfall because I chose to put it away to fix the retaining wall on our creek. I could not do it all, not because I'm stupid or bad with money, but because that's the economic reality.

Third, commit to not second-guessing yourself. This is important because of the psychological principle of adaptation: We adjust to whatever we experience regularly. In other words, over time, we tend to take for granted what we have, no matter how wonderful, and the joy we experienced at what we chose tends to fade. As a result, regret tends to increase as we start to believe the other choice would have made us happier. That's where gratitude comes in. When you consciously focus on the good aspects of the choice you've made rather than the "if onlys" on the road not taken, you'll be happier with your decisions.

When I see red Volkswagen turbo convertibles go by (my car of choice), I could spend the rest of my days wishing I had bought one instead of fixing the creek. Instead I remember how grateful I am that I can now afford to fix the wall—it will add value to my property if I want to sell and give me tremendous peace of mind when it rains. It will mean that we can live here safely for decades if we choose. The more you appreciate and enjoy the choice you did make, the less regret you will experience.

Finally, it helps, Schwartz notes, to "remember just how complex life is and to realize how rare it is that any single decision, in and of itself, has the life-transforming power we sometimes think," he writes. If you find yourself deep in regret over choices you made long ago, remember that the story you are telling yourself about what marvelous things would have come to pass if you'd only made the other choice is just that—a story. In reality, you have no idea where that choice would have led. Rather than regretting the choices you didn't make, follow the advice of Smiley Blanton, "To be happy, drop the words *if only* and substitute instead the words *next time*." Take the lesson from your sense of regret, but leave the pain behind.

14

Does Perfectionism Have You in Its Grip?

"Excellence doesn't require perfection."
—*Henry James*

Marsha asked me to help her learn to be happier. She was incredibly hardworking and demanding of herself and those who worked for her. Any time she or anyone around her made a mistake, she would go ballistic. She would berate herself for missing the ball in a tennis game and her teammates for failing to anticipate everything that could go wrong in a product launch. She would go over and over each mistake—*how could (I/they) have done such a thing?*—until she became such a black cloud that, even though she was incredibly talented, people would go out of their way to avoid working with her.

Marsha was suffering from perfectionism, a terrible happiness destroyer that confuses excellence with never making a mistake. In a way, perfectionists have got it backward. They can't be satisfied with anything less than a "10," but when they do fall short, their harsh response deprives them of knowledge that would actually help them improve. More and more, research is showing that at birth, the brain is "wired" to track success and discard failure. But perfectionists focus exclusively on failure—*you didn't do it right, you idiot*—so they continue to be stuck. There are serious consequences for such behavior. Research has shown that perfectionists are less healthy, less happy, have less satisfying relationships, and even earn less than others.

I helped Marsha see that underneath her perfectionism lay a healthy desire for excellence. And that excellence is created by learning from our errors. Rather than beating herself or others up when something went wrong, she began to ask, "What can I/we learn here so that this doesn't happen again? What system or process or understanding can I/we put in place so that this can be excellent?" Because her standard became excellence, not perfection, and she allowed herself to learn, Marsha began to enjoy whatever she was doing more, which created even more excellence. Soon people wanted to be on her team because it was not only producing great results, but also folks were having fun. And Marsha became happier with herself and the people around her.

In his book *Happiness Is a Choice,* Barry Neil Kaufman refers to the "mistakes wheel," an adaptation of the Native American medicine wheel. The five categories are: In the north, "Learning from our own mistakes." In the west, "Learning from the mistakes of others." In the east, "Learning from the mistakes of our teachers." In the south, "Being willing to make as many mistakes as it takes." And in the center: "Learning that there is no such thing as a mistake."

How do you treat yourself when you or someone else makes a mistake? Can you learn from the mistake wheel? Baseball greats Hank Aaron and Babe Ruth led not only in home runs, but also in strikeouts because they swung at the ball more than other players. The more you allow for errors, the better results you will produce in your life. And the happier you'll be.

15

Do You Always
Have to Be Right?

"This very moment is a seed from which the
flowers of tomorrow's happiness grow."
—*Margaret Lindsey*

The Ryan family motto, at least as it was translated from
the Latin to me, is "I'd rather die than give in." And I certainly lived that way, at least when it came to intimate
relationships. Whenever there was a conflict between me
and my significant other, I would leave no stone unturned
in proving I was right. If that meant hurtful words, raised
voice, threats, it didn't matter. I was out to win.

The first time someone said to me, "Would you rather
be right or happy?" it annoyed me to no end. *I'll be happy
when he realizes I'm right,* I thought to myself. Why does
it have to be either/or?

But over time, I've come to see the wisdom of that old
saw. If you burn down the house, anger your colleagues,
and alienate your children in your quest, you may be right,
but you most likely will be homeless, jobless, and loveless.
Or at least not truly happy.

One of the problems with having to be right is that in
order for you to win, someone must lose—and no one likes

to feel like a loser. It certainly isn't conducive to healthy and happy work and family relationships. But at a deeper level, the problem with being right is that it narrows our focus so that all we can see is our need to win and we lose sight of the pain we're causing, the consequences of our actions, or even whether what we're arguing about matters all that much to us. Swept up by the need for victory, we lose touch with whether it's something worth winning, and at what price.

That's why, when I find myself getting all worked up in self-righteousness, I ask myself, "What's really important to me here?" It helps me remember my true priorities— whether that's the issue I'm worked up about or a deeper commitment to being loving, kind, patient, for instance. From that place, I can decide how hard to press my case or even whether it's worth making a big deal about at all.

Solutions in conflict are not necessarily easy. Sometimes important values clash, even within yourself. At least when you ask yourself what's important, you make visible to yourself what you're really fighting about. And when you ask the other person the same question, it helps to find common ground and increases the possibility of finding a solution that makes everyone happy.

I was once called in to mediate between feuding business partners. Each was trying to convince the other that she was right and the other one wrong in the way they were going about building their business. Rather than listen to the merits of each case, I asked them both to tell me what they cared about in relation to the business. Each spoke passionately about her sense of mission and how dedicated she was to making it work. "So what's important to both of you," I said, "is making the business a success. But if you keep feuding, you will destroy it. How can you look at this problem together so that what's really important to you is preserved?" They got it—and were able to find solutions that had never occurred to either of them when they were insistent on being right.

This choice to remember what's important is a crucial one when we want to be happy. For inevitably, as we go about our daily lives, we will bump into other people who do things that annoy or frustrate us. The way we treat them—and ourselves—moment to moment has consequences to our happiness, not only in the here and now, but in the future.

The ways we act toward others now are the seeds of our future happiness. Remembering what's truly important in any given moment helps us keep the implications of our actions front and center.

16

Do You Need to Adjust Your Happiness Set Point?

> "You can have anything you want if you want it desperately enough. You must want it with an inner exuberance that erupts through the skin and joins the energy that created the world."
>
> —*Sheila Graham*

"You know," Elizabeth confided in me the other day when I spoke to her about this book, "I get an anxious feeling in the pit of my stomach when I feel too happy. And I'm constantly going around telling my kids to settle down if they get too excited or happy. What's that about?"

I knew exactly what she was talking about. I'd noticed it in myself as well. If Don gets too exuberant, I get slightly agitated and tell him to calm down. And I rarely feel excitement or raucous high spirits. I've always thought of it like the governor on a motor—the governor controls how fast or slow the engine idles. If –5 is feeling terrible most of the time, and +5 is the kind of zest Sheila Graham is referring to, I've always thought of mine as idling at around 1. (And that is an improvement—before I learned the things in this book, I would have put myself down at –2 or –3.) Other people seem to have a much higher set point, able to feel and express great joy and enthusiasm, embracing life with a passionate gusto that I could only stand in awe of. And research on those who've won big money in the lottery as well as those who become suddenly paralyzed has shown that we each do have a happiness set point that we tend to return to regardless of good or bad fortune. But I never knew where the difference might come from.

Then I read Dr. Susan C. Vaughan's book *Half Empty, Half Full*. And there was the answer. It turns out that if all goes well during the first year of life, through interactions with our primary caretakers, we learn to experience and amplify positive emotions such as elation and pleasure. Eye contact, tossing in the air, tickling, smiling, and laughing together—through such activities the "mother senses the baby's affective state, meets and matches his mood where it is at the moment, then nudges the baby's mood into a slightly more expansive, joyful place by conveying a slightly broader positive response. Her goal is to push the envelope, to encourage the infant to go right up to the edge, when it comes to the intensity of feeling he can tolerate."

In so doing, a strong loop between our limbic system (our emotional brain) and our cortex (our thinking brain) gets created, fueled by the neurotransmitter dopamine, "which is known to be important in pleasure- and reward-seeking behaviors throughout life." These experiences with the outside world "eventually form the internal cortical reins that steer the limbic system toward a happier, more joyful state... What we are actually encoding in these early life experiences is the *process* of our interactions with Mom."

But things can go wrong. Caretakers must have the capacity for attunement for the process to work, and because of their early childhood experiences they may lack this ability. Depressed mothers, for instance, do not smile or laugh with their children as much and infants who don't get positive amplification eventually give up. And if parents themselves were not amplified as infants, they can get agitated at the exuberance of their children and seek to calm them down rather than rev them up. Thus, when we begin to get excited or elated as adults, we treat ourselves as our parents did—we feel we're doing something wrong and bring ourselves down.

So are we doomed to our happiness set point, whatever it is? There is much more research into how to work with negative mood states in order to be happier than there is on how to amplify positive moods. And my own experience and that of my clients is more about negative mood modulation. However, if we can think ourselves out of bad spots, we can think ourselves up as well.

To begin, notice what your set point is. Can you easily experience positive emotions? Or does it make you anxious? Rate it on a scale of –5 to +5. Then decide what you want your number to be. Make a mental commitment to thinking up. When you notice yourself feeling uncomfortable or agitated when you or someone else starts to feel up, remind yourself that it's not dangerous and challenge yourself to let it rip.

That's what I've been doing and so far so good. Twice this week, I laughed so hard I cried. It felt great and nothing bad happened!

17

What about Biochemistry?

"In addition to my other numerous acquaintances, I have one more intimate confidant. My depression is the most faithful mistress I have known— no wonder, then, that I return the love."

—*Søren Kierkegaard*

I was talking to my friend Kathy about this book. She looked at me and asked, "But what about people whose biochemistry won't let them be happy?" Yes, biochemical imbalances are real and so is depression. Antidepressants have helped a lot of people, in the words of a suffering friend, "feel like there's a bottom to the pit." I'm not a medical professional and I make no medical or moral judgment about those who choose to get chemical support. The ideas in this book are for nondepressed folks or those who may be depressed and want to learn some attitudinal ways of becoming happier with or without drugs.

Whether it's learned behavior or innate biochemistry that's bringing us down is in some senses irrelevant. Research shows that our thoughts become our biochemistry as they flood our bodies with upper or downer hormones. For instance, two University of Pittsburgh psychologists counted the ratio of good and bad thoughts in depressed and happy people. What they discovered is that depressed folks have one bad thought for every one good one; nondepressed people have two good thoughts for every negative one. Depressed people who improve move to the 2:1 ratio; those who stay down remain at 1:1.

The implications are obvious—change your thoughts and your mood will change. There are a variety of therapeutic approaches to depression that work on this principle of mind training. They are very similar to the ideas in this book: becoming aware of thoughts that bring us down, challenging negative thinking, and creating alternative positive thoughts.

If you try a lot of ideas in this or other books and your unhappiness is persistent, you may want to see a qualified medical professional about whether you are suffering from clinical depression and may benefit from some psychotropic drug. Experts claim that the very best treatment for depression is a combination of drugs and behavioral/attitudinal change. Or you may be suffering from thyroid problems or severe PMS. A good doctor can help with hormonal challenges to happiness.

A sense of general well-being is our birthright. You deserve to feel as good as possible as much as possible.

III

ACTIVATING DAILY HAPPINESS

"It is only possible to live happily-ever-after on a day-to-day basis."

—*Margaret Bonnano*

I once read a quote by Hugh Downs that said, "A happy person is not a person in a certain set of circumstances, but rather a person with a certain set of attitudes." We only have to compare two people in the exact same circumstances—one happy, one not—to know just how true Hugh Downs's comment is. But no matter what our negative mental habits up till now, we can cultivate the thoughts and behaviors that promote feeling happier on a daily basis.

That's what this section provides—the best set of practices I've learned to create the neurological pathway to your left prefrontal cortex, where the experience of happiness—satisfaction, contentment, fulfillment—resides. That way, when you notice yourself headed down the tired old path to misery, you can stop, employ one of these ideas, and head to happiness instead.

It's okay if you don't *feel* happy to begin with. As research psychologist David G. Myers points out, "We are as likely to *act our way into a new way of thinking* as to think ourselves into a new way of acting," he notes in *The Pursuit of Happiness*. The more you practice, the more the positive feelings will follow.

18

Recognize That
Your Happiness Is
Your Own Responsibility

"Perhaps the biggest source of unhappiness...
stems from the idea that there is someone
out there who will meet all our needs,
because it turns us into needful children,
waiting to be fed... We are not vessels in
need of filling up, we are persons in our
own right with resources of our own."

—*Merle Shain*

Years ago, I took a communications workshop with my then partner, Will. It was standard advice about "speaking from I, not you," and so forth. I found it useful and true, and was glad I did it. Except for one thing—we were taught to take responsibility for our own feelings. As the leader pointed out, no one can make us feel anything. Our feelings may be in response to another person's behavior, but the responsibility for them lies with us.

You were supposed to say things like "When you didn't call when you said you would, I felt abandoned" rather than "You made me mad when you didn't call." I couldn't do it. With all my heart I believed Will was responsible for making me happy or miserable, and I would not let go of that belief. If he called or came home on time, if he bought me the right kind of present, if he paid enough attention, I would be happy. Otherwise I would be miserable, and it would be all his fault. You might guess I wasn't often happy and our relationship was filled with strife.

It took decades and our breaking up and my not wanting to repeat the painful past for this belief to finally shake loose. By observing the wide range of responses by others to the same event, I finally got it that my feelings were my own—true to me, and created by me from an amalgam of my past and my current response to someone's behavior. They were *my* responsibility, as was my happiness. I could make requests for certain behaviors, but how I chose to respond to another person's behavior was my own business that determined my happiness in that moment.

A simple example. I love orderliness in the house, and I live with two people who love to collect stuff and leave it everywhere. I can ask them to pick up after themselves, which they claim to do. But their idea of picking up does not come even close to matching my standards. I could pitch a fit every day about how they make me miserable with their messes. I could leave their stuff all over and fume every time I see it. But because I know my happiness is my responsibility, I choose to tidy up myself by putting all their stuff into their respective rooms, where they can choose to clean it up or leave it a mess. That way I have order in the rest of the house, which brings me pleasure, and keep the harmony between the three of us, which allows me to enjoy them more and feel better about myself.

I've gotten so much happier since I've stopped trying to get others to make me happy. If my husband buys me a wonderful present, great! If he forgets Valentine's Day, I focus on the opportunity to love him anyway and ask him to try to remember the next time (which usually results in a gift the next day rather than a bitter fight that leaves us disconnected for weeks). I've finally got the keys to the safety deposit box of happiness in my own heart—and boy, does taking responsibility for myself feel good.

19

Remember, You're Not Responsible for Anyone Else's Happiness— Including Your Kids'

"No one is really responsible to make someone
else happy, no matter what most people
have been taught and accept as true."

—*Sidney Madwed*

The phone rang at 2 p.m. It was Ana, calling from her summer program. "Tiera and Mia won't play with me," she wailed. "I want you to come and bring me home." I felt a giant tug on my heartstrings—my child was unhappy. The mother lion in me rose up—how mean those girls were! Of course I'd come right over—and give those two an earful on the way out!

Then I stopped for a moment. What message would I send seven-year-old Ana if I ran to the rescue? That she was powerless to solve her own problems. That she must look to others for her happiness. But I knew she needed a bit of support—simply telling her to resolve it for herself wouldn't work. If she could have, she wouldn't have called. So I asked her about the trouble she was having. "I don't know why they won't play with me," she proclaimed, "and I won't ask." Sensing a dead end, I tried another approach. "Look around the room. What are the other kids doing?"

"Well, some kids are beading," she replied. "Some are doing art and others playing Legos."

"Do you think you could join one of those groups?" I asked.

"Yes," she responded, hanging up the phone.

When I arrived at the regular pickup time at five, she was her usual cheerful self. I asked her how she'd solved her problem. "Well," she said, "I just gave up and did something else."

I've often written that Ana is one of my greatest teachers. That day, she proved to me that while I may think my job as a parent is to make her happy, my real task is to help her figure out how to make herself happy.

The same is true for the adults in our lives. We can help them think about how to expand their options when they're stuck, support them when they take risks, point out the effects they are having on us. But it's not our job to make them happy, even if by some miracle we could.

However, there's something about love, at least in this culture, that makes us think we're supposed to. We take our loved ones' unhappiness personally, even when it has nothing to do with us. We bend ourselves into knots, jump through hoops, give up what is near and dear to us in an attempt to "make" them happy. I know women who devote every waking hour to meeting the wants of their spouses. I've seen a man move twelve times in twelve years for the sake of an unhappy wife. I've seen parents cater to their children's every whim. But I've never met a person who has become happy as a consequence of such actions. Dependent? Yes. Self-centered? Yes. Temporarily victorious? Yes. But happy? Never, because happiness cannot be granted by one person to another. It is earned through our choosing to embrace all the beauty life has to offer and using all of who we are for a purpose we deem worthwhile. And that is something we do for ourselves.

The effect on the giver isn't good either. Most often, you end up resentful as your attempts fail. Or your love fades as you burn out in exhaustion and despair.

This doesn't mean that you shouldn't care about the feelings of those around you. Or that you never offer counsel or support, or compromise for someone you love. Simply that you recognize that the responsibility for happiness resides inside each of us. When we love, we hold the beloved in tender hands, supporting their growth toward happiness but never making ourselves the granter of it.

Declare your emotional independence—your happiness is your own responsibility and so it is for everyone else.

20

Know That
Everyone Wants
to Be Happy

"If you want others to be happy,
practice compassion. If you want to
be happy, practice compassion."

—*The Dalai Lama*

I first heard Buddhist monk Thich Nhat Hanh speak right after the Rodney King beatings. Someone had asked him about the incident. His first reply, in his typical soft-spoken way, was, "Poor Rodney King." But then he said something that changed my life. "Poor policemen—what suffering they must have experienced in their lives to treat someone like that."

That sentence was a wake-up call. Before that, I had the world neatly divided into the good camp—people who think and act like me—and the bad camp—those who intentionally do things to make me and others miserable. What Thich Nhat Hanh was saying was that at heart, all people are good and they do bad things out of ignorance or as a consequence of the suffering they themselves have experienced.

As I studied Buddhism more, I came to understand that there was a belief at its core that had tremendous implications: namely, that all beings want to be happy and all human actions are attempts to be happy. This doesn't mean we do it well, this doesn't mean that we don't create great suffering for ourselves or others. Just that our intention is to be happy. Indeed, one of the ways Buddhists develop compassion for others is by recognizing this common desire for happiness: Just as I want to be happy, so do all beings.

It isn't only Buddhists who hold this perspective. St. Augustine of Hippo wrote the same thing in the third century: "Everyone, whatever his condition, desires to be happy. There is no one who does not desire this, and each one desires it with such earnestness that it is preferred to all things."

This awareness has had profound implications in my life. My heart opens kindly toward myself when I realize all I really want is to be happy, even if I'm messing up in the moment. And my heart also goes out to all those people known and unknown in the world who are all striving for the same thing. This doesn't mean I allow myself to be harmed by others, but simply that I recognize our commonality and therefore my peace of mind is not as disturbed when they do something I don't like. When a stranger is rude, I think, he's just trying to be happy, as I am. When a client or coworker does something I disapprove of, I think, he's just trying to be happy, as I am. I may disapprove of the way someone is going about trying to be happy, but when I remember that everyone just wants to be happy, their clumsy means don't disrupt my happiness as much.

Everyone wants to be happy. How can we do it in such a way that increases joy and decreases suffering in ourselves and others? How do we use our desire for happiness to connect us more deeply to one another? How can we treat ourselves and others compassionately as we stumble toward happiness? These are profound questions not to be answered lightly, but lived into.

The closest I've come in my understanding is to try and be as kind as possible to myself and those I meet. For as the Dalai Lama points out in the above quote, there is an inextricable relationship between happiness and kindness.

Here's how Scott Morrison puts it in *Open and Innocent: The Gentle, Passionate Art of Not-Knowing*:

Do you really want to be happy? Just... be kind, unconditionally kind, on this breath alone. Forget about the future. Just this breath. No matter the circumstances, just be kind. Friend, lover, family member, someone who seems to hate you, someone you've never met on the street, your own soft animal body. Just be kind, in whatever way is appropriate.

In practicing compassion—for ourselves and others— said the Buddha, we experience gladness and delight. I do know that the more I try to treat others well, the happier I feel.

21

Find Ways to Use
Your Full Powers

"The ancient Greek definition of
happiness was the full use of your
powers along lines of excellence."
—*John F. Kennedy*

Elòn Graham is a fourteen-year-old boy who lives with
his single mom in Berkeley, California. Even when very
young, he wouldn't touch the fast food his mom prefers.
At two he was asking for broccoli, and by seven he was
whipping up salads and entrees for his dinner. This year,
he got the idea to create a cookbook for kids. He cooked,
and his grandma wrote down what he did. He's now selling his work, with the proceeds going to a rescue mission.

I found out about Elòn through a profile in the *San
Francisco Chronicle*. About to enter high school, he dreams
of becoming a professional chef. Neither his mother nor
grandmother can explain where his cooking passion
comes from.

Elòn is a sterling example of how we each come into
the world with certain unique talents. Elòn was just lucky
to discover his while young and to have a family that supported their cultivation. Gifts like musical or mathematical

ability are obvious. But we all have gifts whether we recognize them as talents or not—a penchant for understanding others' feelings, for instance, or getting people excited about doing something, or being able to see what could go wrong in a situation.

In research on a sample of two million people around the world, the Gallup organization discovered that each of us has five or six of these unique talents, and that the more we understand and cultivate them, the more excellent and successful we become. And the more we use them, the more fulfilled we feel.

Fulfillment is the kind of happiness Kennedy is referring to in the quote above—the sense of using yourself the way you were meant to. The great short story writer Flannery O'Connor, who battled lupus her whole adult life and died from it at age thirty-nine, was often asked why she wrote despite her illness. "Because I'm good at it," was her habitual response. When we are using our talents, we feel like racehorses who are allowed to run as fast as they can.

This source of happiness is available at any moment when we deploy our talents. It just feels great, like Elòn feels when cooking. Unfortunately, for a lot of us, certain assumptions and experiences stand in the way of our experiencing this happiness. We may take our talents for granted, not seeing them as gifts. I once knew a woman who believed that her talent for optimism was of no use in business at all! I could not convince her that having someone who could see the positives could add value to a work team. Or perhaps, like my friend Dawna, who has a talent for storytelling but was always accused of exaggerating when young, you've been criticized or ridiculed for your talents.

As a culture, we tend to value certain gifts—artistic, athletic, or financial ability in particular—and not even consider others as talents at all—the capacity for developing others, for example, or being able to create harmony. As a consequence, we can end up envying others' talents and denigrating our own.

When I was in my twenties and feeling that I had no true talents to cultivate, I had an experience that changed my life. I was talking to my painter friend Michael. I was saying that what he did was a true talent and I wished I were talented. He went into his studio and laid out twelve versions of the same scene he'd been working on. "Which one is best?" he asked. I pointed to one. "Yes," he said, "and knowing that is your talent." From that moment on, I stopped pooh-poohing my gift of discernment and went on to create a career as an editor that made me happy for twenty-five years.

Finding and using your talents is a crucial key to personal happiness. One of the greatest investors of all time, John Marks Templeton, put it this way: "Success depends more on how you develop your talents than on how many talents you have." He advises asking yourself: "Am I doing the thing that I am best qualified to do?"

Perhaps your talents are invisible to you so you don't know the answer to Templeton's question. If you need help identifying them, you can find an assessment available on my website—*www.mj-ryan.com*—along with specific ideas on how to use your particular talents more. The more you cultivate your full powers, the more your life will feel worth living.

22

Before Freaking Out, Wait for the End of the Story

> "I would die happy if I knew that on my tombstone could be written these words, This man was an absolute fool. None of the disastrous things that he reluctantly predicted ever came to pass!"
>
> —*Lewis Mumford*

I live on a creek. In the California winters when it rains for weeks, the creek rises and my house is so close that the roaring water is only a few yards from my bedroom. After enduring four winters of this, I decided that I wanted to build a better retaining wall so that I would not have to worry so much that the house would fall in.

Simple enough, right? Well, not exactly. Two years and umpteen thousands spent, we still don't have the permit. It's a complex process involving the state, the federal government, and the county. And estimates of the cost fluctuate wildly, as do the conditions for building: It can only be done in September, only if you use certain rocks... Believe me, you don't want to know it all.

The process has been grueling, but instructive. As a chronic worrier, I have been looking for decades for ways to stop worrying so that I could be happier. And the saga of the creek wall has finally provided it. There have been so many ups and downs, so many tens of thousands taken away and added on, that I finally just decided not to get involved in all the twists and turns and simply wait for the end of the story. Something will be built. It will cost something. We will figure out how to pay for it or add it to our mortgage. Until we know, I refuse to get all worked up about it.

Boy, have I been happier since I came to this place. And not just about the creek—I've decided not to get worked up about *anything* until I get to the end of the story. When I find myself worrying about my daughter's reading ability, for instance, I remind myself it's not the end of the story and we have time to work on it. When I start worrying about getting more clients, I remind myself that it's not the end of the story and I have enough right now.

Waiting for the end of the story does two things. It keeps you from catastrophizing all the possible things that could go wrong that most likely will never come to pass. And it allows you to put what is happening into some kind of perspective so you can be happier in the moment, no matter what is going on.

There's a famous Taoist story that illustrates the importance of such perspective. I've seen dozens of variations, but here's one I like. A poor farmer has his horse stolen. His neighbors express their sympathy at his misfortune. The farmer replies, "How do you know this isn't a good thing?" A few months pass and the horse returns, bringing a mate. Soon the farmer has many horses and becomes very rich. The neighbors exclaim over his good luck. The farmer replies, "How do you know this isn't a bad thing?" One day, the farmer's son goes riding on their finest horse, falls, breaks his hip, and becomes permanently lame. The neighbors arrive to offer their condolences. To which the farmer replies, "How do you know this isn't a good thing?" Soon war comes to the region and all the ablebodied young men are sent out to fight. Nine out of ten die. The farmer's son, because he is lame, has stayed home and lives to a ripe old age in great prosperity.

What this fable teaches us is that the story is really never over. It goes on and on, with each chapter seemingly offering something to get worked up over. "As long as life exists," writes Robert Fulghum in *All I Really Need to Know I Learned in Kindergarten,* "something always happens next." If we take the long view, we can move more gracefully through the chapters, knowing that even that which seems painful or difficult can lead to happiness. And when we are in a happy phase, we can relish it all the more, knowing that inevitably, because everything in life is impermanent, another chapter will come along. So we might as well wring as much joy from this moment as we can.

23

When Faced with an Obstacle, Change, Leave, or Allow—with Grace

"Every day give yourself a good
mental shampoo."

—*Sara Jordan*

Born in 1884, Sara Murray Jordan became a gastroenter-ologist and one of the four founders of the world-famous Lahey Clinic in Boston, Massachusetts. A graduate of Radcliffe College in 1904, she went on to receive a Ph.D. from the University of Munich and an M.D. from Tufts. She was given many honorary degrees from universities around the world for her pioneering research and served at the Lahey Clinic until her death in 1958. She succeeded tremendously at a time when women were typically house-wives and in a field that was exceedingly competitive and male dominated. Clearly she didn't allow such obstacles to interfere with her goals.

I believe Jordan knew the formula for happiness that my friend Dawna Markova, author of *I Will Not Die an Unlived Life*, has recently been teaching me. When faced with a situation that is interfering with our happiness, we have three options: (1) Change it with grace; (2) Leave with grace; or (3) Allow or accept it with grace. The trick is first to understand that those are our choices (rather than moaning or complaining, for instance).

Then we must decide which of the three options is most preferable and doable with grace. That's where the mental shampoo comes in. We need to clean our minds of feelings of victimization or anger so we can choose well. The more gracefully we behave in enacting our choice, the less havoc we leave in our wake and the happier we feel.

That, I believe, was something Sara Jordan understood. She accepted that she was the only woman in her medical school instead of letting that prevent her from attending. She changed various forms of treatment for gastrointestinal disorders because she wasn't satisfied with the standard ones. And she left her first husband and remarried even though social convention at the time was strongly against divorce.

When you understand that if you want to be happy, these really are your only options, life gets much simpler. Every time you find yourself frustrated by something or someone, you just ask yourself if this is something you can change with grace, want to leave with grace, or must allow with grace. Any other choice is a choice to remain stuck in misery, fear, or bitterness. For instance, my husband drives me crazy by not keeping the house tidy when I travel; dead flowers left in vases is one of my pet peeves. Can I change him? Not likely. I've asked and he does the best he can. Should I leave him? If he were an abuser or an addict, sure, but a dead flower hoarder? If I want to live happily with him, I must accept him with grace, as he is.

This truth is what's at the heart of the Serenity Prayer of AA and many other spiritual approaches to life: If you want to be happier, know what you can and can't control. Change what you can and accept the rest.

It's important to realize that this is a practice for happiness, not for being right. Is it "right" that Don doesn't throw away the dead flowers and clean the house thoroughly? Probably not—everyone should be able to pick up after themselves. But this isn't about the moral high ground. It's about being happy on a daily basis. Was it "right" that Sara Jordan had to succeed in a man's world without female support around her? I bet she didn't even entertain the question. She was too busy choosing what would make her the happiest under the circumstances.

Next time you are annoyed or upset, give yourself a mental shampoo and look at the three options. Which will increase your happiness the most? Which can you do with grace? The choice is yours.

24

Figure Out What Really Matters to You

"Happiness is that state of consciousness which proceeds from the achievement of one's values."

—*Ayn Rand*

Barb is an artist who has been working steadily at her craft for almost thirty years. She doesn't make a whole lot of money, but that never stops her. I've watched her over the decades; she's a great example of someone who is committed to something and keeps at it, despite little reward or recognition.

Recently she sent me a note saying that she has finally discovered her key to happiness as an artist—shows she puts together at her house with self-imposed deadlines. She explained, "My happiness seems to arrive when I know that everything I am doing feeds into the sharing of my work with friends and community. By scheduling two open studios a year, I do not get depressed about my work. I am receiving regular recognition in the community, which helps keep me happier." Barb is happy because she figured out what really matters to her—to keep working, to share her work with others—and what structures—the open studios—would support her getting it.

Barb is married to Bill, a public health doctor. He also knows what matters to him—to putter in his garden, to play the piano, to eat great food, to have a vacation to look forward to—and has structured his life around these pursuits. While he enjoys his work, without these other things, he would not be as cheerful.

Each of us has certain things we really need to be happy. Many of us think it's a new car or a fancy house, but research into happy people reveals that a key component of happiness is the ability to identify our true needs and then to make it a priority to pursue them.

The more I work with folks, the more I've come to see that what we truly need is a life that expresses our values. Our values are the things in life that really matter to us, whatever they may be. They are not things that can be dictated from the outside by our governments, churches, or parents. They are completely personal. Barb values artistic expression and sharing what she has done with others; Bill values music, gardening, and travel. My friend Andy values beauty and is unhappy unless he lives in a natural environment. I value close, intimate relationships and the cultivation of wisdom. If I did not have opportunities to live those values I would not be happy, regardless of how much money I might make or how many trips I might take.

If you are not as happy as you want, perhaps you are not aware enough of your values. If so, try this practice inspired by lifestyle guru Alexandra Stoddard. Put pen to paper and, without stopping, write down the first seven words that come to your mind when you think of what really matters to you. Here's my list: wisdom, integrity, warm weather, intimacy, sleep, helping others grow, security.

You can also check out *www.authentichappiness. org* and take the Values in Action (VIA) inventory. It's also called the Signature Strengths inventory. It's a way of understanding what you deeply care about (and what you don't—humor and playfulness scored at the very bottom of my list, which is why I often see my husband, who scores high on playfulness, as being frivolous). As Martin Seligman, creator of the site and the book that goes along with it, notes, activation of our values "produces authentic positive emotion in the doer: pride, satisfaction, joy, fulfillment, or harmony." The more we find ways to live our values on a daily basis, the more satisfied with our lives we'll be.

Want proof? In a study cited on their website, a group of people were asked to use their VIAs more often and in different ways. These folks were happier six months later as compared to a control group who stayed the same.

25

Shine the Flashlight on What's Right

"Some people are always grumbling
because roses have thorns; I am
thankful that thorns have roses."

—*Alphonse Karr*

A few years ago, I read an article that demonstrated the power of looking at what's right in creating happiness. It was about a young teenager who kept running away from home. Her parents wanted her declared a delinquent and placed in juvenile hall. Instead, the courts sentenced her to meet with a community group for six months. They in turn gave her an assignment—to come every week with a list of what was right about her home and family. She now is living happily at home. I assume that her home was the same before and after. What changed was that before she made the list, she had shone the flashlight of attention on all that she disliked about the situation and was therefore miserable. After, she pointed it at what was right and was happy.

Focusing on what's right is so powerful an agent for positive change that a whole new business field of organizational development called Appreciative Inquiry has sprung up to investigate and expand this notion. A search for the best in people and systems, the foundations of Appreciative Inquiry include the "positive principle," as James D. Ludema calls it, which holds that "human beings and organizations move in the direction of what they study. [T]he more positive the topics of inquiry and the more positive the questions asked, the more positive will be the 'theories' we come to discover." In other words, look for problems and you will find them. Look for what's working and you will find that.

According to the Appreciative Inquiry website, *appreciate* means "valuing; the act of recognizing the best in people or the world around us; affirming past and present strengths, successes, and potentials; to perceive those things that give life (health, vitality, excellence)."

Have you caught the connection to personal happiness? The more we recognize and affirm our strengths, successes, and potentials, and the more we know the things that give us health, vitality, and excellence, the more fulfilling our lives are and the happier we feel moment to moment. The energy of noticing what's right creates excitement to move forward, like plants turning toward the light. Like the young girl who changed her feelings about home, often when we look at what's right, we experience contentment with things just as they are.

When we pay attention to our failures, mistakes, and flaws, however, we only know what's not right. I often meet folks who say, I don't know what I want, I just know I don't want this. As they've experienced, focusing on what's wrong doesn't help them move toward anything, nor does it create the uprush of positive emotion that we experience as happiness. They feel demoralized, de-energized, depressed.

This is not to say that we should never look at a problem. But once you've done that, it's time to focus on the positive to find the solution—and more happiness. So if a project or relationship is stuck, once you've recognized that, it's best to ask yourself questions like: *What could be right about this situation? When have I dealt with something like this successfully in the past? What did I do then? What's the best outcome I can imagine here? What do I need to do to make that happen?*

For instance, a friend is trying to sell her house and has no takers. When I asked her what could be right about this, she said she was very impatient and this seemed to be a way for her to learn patience. Now, every time she finds herself getting frustrated about the sale, she remembers that it's a patience test and challenges herself to be grateful for the opportunity to learn.

Focusing on what's right gives us hope and energy.

26

To Touch the 10,000 Joys, Be Willing to Touch the 10,000 Sorrows

"The word 'happiness' would lose its meaning if it were not balanced by sadness."

—*Carl Jung*

Rick Foster and Greg Hicks are business consultants who, several years ago, began to study happiness. They did it by asking folks who was the happiest person they knew, having those people rate themselves on a scale of happiness and provide referrals to others who could validate their happiness, and then interviewing those with the highest scores.

Sheri was a self-proclaimed happy person they encountered in their search. When they asked her about how she handled the most difficult situation in her life, she proceeded to describe her mother's attempted suicide when Sheri was nine. Her father made her mop up the blood all over the walls and floors because she was the oldest. She reported that she dealt with it by repressing the memory for thirty years and now never thinking about it, because there's "no point in rehashing it... The best way to deal with stuff is to stay positive. That's why I'm so happy."

Foster and Hicks didn't experience Sheri as happy. They found her cold and distant, in denial of her pain and thus cut off from her feelings. "Her denial is not happiness," they write, "it's numbness."

In contrast, they discovered that all the truly happy people they encountered "dive into negative feelings head on and experience them deeply... They don't censor raw emotion, deny feelings or run from pain as many of us do in an attempt to 'move on.' "This doesn't mean that they stay there forever. Eventually happy people "begin to transform their feelings with new reactions and insights. What lessons can they learn? What new meaning can they create for their lives?"

But first they are willing to experience, rather than avoid, the emotional pain that life dishes out. In Buddhism there is the belief that life is full of "10,000 joys and 10,000 sorrows," as I have heard author Jack Kornfield describe it. In order to experience the 10,000 joys, he often says, you must be willing also to touch the 10,000 sorrows. Otherwise, like Sheri, you are numb to life. Human existence is both dark and light; we can't really have one without the other. Our capacity for enthusiasm and vitality is only as deep as our ability to experience vulnerability and loss. Indeed, it is precisely because we experience vulnerability along with joy that we don't take it for granted, but treasure it as the fragile, beautifully rare gift it is.

My wise friend Daphne Rose Kingma, author of many books, once said of someone we both know, "He wants to go through life without life going through him." That's another way of saying the same thing. Life *does* go through us as we go through it, and we are meant to be transformed as a consequence. The more we allow life—in all its complexity, with all its sorrows and joys—to go through us, the more we grow in depth and dimension, and the greater our capacity to withstand grief and feel profound joy.

Experiencing great pain or sorrow is survivable only if we use it to teach us something worthwhile. Otherwise, it's unmitigated torture. That's why it's so important for our ultimate happiness when we go through hardships to ask ourselves questions such as one that Hicks and Foster use in their book *How We Choose to Be Happy:* "As difficult or painful as the problem may be, what things of great importance have I learned about myself (or others) because of this problem?" When we learn from our pain, we transform from victims to victors, giving meaning to our suffering and breaking open to life's joyfulness as well as its sorrows.

27

Be Happy
for Everyone Else's Sake

"Remember that happiness is as contagious as
gloom. It should be the first duty of those who
are happy to let others know of their gladness."
—*Maurice Maeterlinck*

Recently I was at Esalen to teach a workshop. Another
offering at the same time was "Love Yourself—For
Everyone Else's Sake" by Mark Abramson. I told Mark I
thought it was a brilliant idea. We tend to think that loving
ourselves is selfish or self-entered. However, if we understand we are doing it not for ourselves but for everyone we
meet, then it becomes easier to do.

The same is true for happiness. It may seem self-
indulgent or self-centered to make it a priority in our
lives. Indeed, even now, it feels somewhat frivolous or self-
involved to think that one of my goals in life is to be happy.

But take a moment to think more deeply about it.
When you're unhappy, are you thinking about yourself or
others? Yourself, of course—we tend to be self-involved
when we feel down. The Japanese call it "tone-deaf about
life." That's why Dennis Prager, author of *Happiness Is a
Serious Problem,* says, "Each of us owes it to our spouse,

our children, our friends, to be as happy as we can be. And if you don't believe me, ask a child what it's like to grow up with an unhappy parent, or ask parents what they suffer if they have an unhappy child."

The reason our happiness is so important to those around us is, because of neurobiology, we are constantly being affected by the emotional states of those around us. As Daniel Goleman describes in *Primal Leadership,* our emotional center, the limbic system, is what is known as an open loop system. Rather than being self-regulating like the circulatory system, for instance, an "open-loop system depends largely on external sources to manage itself... In other words, we rely on connections with other people for our own emotional stability." In fact, our feelings are so tuned in to others that the person doesn't even need to be in the same room to be affecting us. Studies done on navy ship commanders, for instance, show that the crew tends to catch the mood of the leader even when he is locked in his own cabin, seemingly not communicating with anyone.

Recently another reason for this mirroring has been discovered. It turns out that we are born with structures in our brains called mirror neurons, which cause us to experience in our bodies other people's emotional intentions even when they say nothing. No one quite knows yet how these work, but the implications are enormous.

Here's how Barry Neil Kaufman puts it in *Happiness Is a Choice:* "What each of us learns has the potential of becoming a message to all humankind... If just one of us changes our beliefs and teaches happiness and love, then that attitude or information goes into the connective tissue of the community and enhances the aptitude for happiness of the entire human group... No single energy can be more impactful on this planet than the joy and well-being emanating from one truly happy and loving person."

So if happiness seems a selfish act, don't do it for yourself—do it for the effect you will have on everyone around you. By choosing to be happy day by day, we have the potential to drive emotions in the positive direction of all those around us—our children and mates, our coworkers and friends, even the people we casually stand next to on the subway. It turns out that happiness truly is contagious.

28

Learn to Think Optimistically

"'There's a light at the end of the tunnel,' says the optimist. 'It's probably a train coming straight at us,' responds the pessimist."
—*David Baird*

I spent the first thirty years of my life as a confirmed pessimist. I figured that if I always looked at things from the bad side, I wouldn't be disappointed. And I wasn't—but I sure wasn't happy either. Finally I got sick of being miserable and decided that life is long and, as *Flow* author Mihaly Csikszentmihalyi said, "It is essential to learn to enjoy life. It really does not make sense to go through the motions of existence if one does not appreciate as much of it as possible." Besides, being pessimistic was the easy way out. It didn't allow for possibility, for change, for hope. I set out consciously to learn to look on the bright side.

Along the way, I learned a few things that have been confirmed by "learned optimism" expert Martin Seligman and others. Optimistic thinkers tend to see negative events as temporary and related to specific events outside their control: *My husband was upset today because of work woes and not because of me. It will be better tomorrow.* Pessimistic folks on the other hand tend to see negative events as permanent, pervasive, and their fault: *I always pick bad men, I'll never be happy again.*

When it comes to positive events, however, optimists and pessimists trade places; optimists see good things as the result of permanent, lasting qualities of themselves: *I did well on the project because I'm smart.* Conversely, pessimists view them as temporary, chance events outside of their control: *I got lucky.* When optimists flunk a test or mess up a project, they assign blame to factors outside of themselves. Because they believe good outcomes are within their control and the bad thing a fluke, they tend to work harder next time to achieve their goal. Conversely, pessimists tend to blame themselves and wonder, what's the use of even trying.

What Seligman and others have shown is that all that's needed to go from being pessimistic to optimistic is to change your explanatory style—the way you explain the good and bad things that happen. There are lots of benefits to doing so. Optimists tend to have happier work and family lives. They stick to things longer and therefore have a greater chance of success. For instance, basketball teams with greater optimism beat their seasonal projected point spread, and optimistic presidential candidates have a greater chance of winning. Thinking optimistically is good for your health too—in a study of 200 Harvard undergraduates over forty years, having a positive attitude at twenty was a predictor of good health at sixty-five, while those who were highly pessimistic at twenty tended at sixty-five to be dead.

Research by David Myers and Ed Diener highlights optimism as one of the key variables in happiness, while age, race, gender, and class turn out not to be predictors at all. So, no matter who you are, when things go well, ask yourself:

- *What about me made this wonderful thing happen?*

And when things go wrong, remind yourself that:

- *The situation is temporary;*
- *It is confined to this one thing;*
- *And it is outside of my control.*

Optimism is really a verb, not a noun. The more we do it, the better we'll feel.

29

Give Yourself a "Why" to Live

"Those who have a 'why' to live,
can bear with almost any 'how.'"

—*Viktor Frankl*

Psychiatrist and author Viktor Frankl didn't just survive German concentration camps, he found his calling there: the creation of a new form of psychotherapy founded on the belief that every person "has his own specific vocation or mission in life; everyone must carry out a concrete assignment that demands fulfillment," as he writes in *Man's Search for Meaning*. The searching for and fulfilling of this mission, he believed, are the reason each of us is alive. When we are on task, we experience a sense of purpose, a sense of what I call "for this I have come," which creates an experience of happiness at its most profound. Through meaning, we find our place in the world and experience our connection to life.

There are many words for this task—mission, vocation, purpose, calling—but the words are less important than the experience, which is the recognition of the connection of your individual life to something greater than mere survival or accumulation of goods. In fact, I've come to believe that the words we use for it actually can get in the way. They loom so large that many of us despair of ever discovering what our unique purpose might be.

Part of the reason is that we fail to understand that this calling comes from our soul and therefore is a mystery to be lived into, not a specific location to be found. We feel deficient that we've never woken up one day and found a map to it in our hand or that we've somehow been given the map but that we're too blind to read it.

In a sense, the continual asking of the question is the answer; as long as we keep wondering, we're navigating closer. I had lunch with a friend recently who articulated this beautifully. "In many ways, I am happier than I've ever been," he said. "I have a great relationship and love what I'm doing. But I keep waking up wondering if this is how I'm supposed to be using my talents. I think I'm sabotaging myself."

"What if," I replied, "the question was kindly rather than a scolding. Is what you're doing how you are supposed to be using your talents?" The more we ask ourselves the question in a friendly curious manner, the closer we'll come to living the answer.

In his posthumously published journal *Markings*, Dag Hammarskjöld, the former secretary general of the United Nations, expresses perfectly the mystery of this journey. "I don't know Who—or What—put the question, I don't know when it was put. I don't even remember answering. But at some moment I did answer Yes to Someone—Something—and from that hour I was certain that existence is meaningful and that, therefore, life, in self-surrender, had a goal."

Another reason issues of purpose are so challenging is that we have glorified work so much in this culture that we think we must find it at the office, that work must be a vehicle not only for making a living, but for making meaning. Certainly millions of people do find meaning through income-producing work, but that is not the aim of business—profit-making is. Meaning is found in all kinds of places, many of them far from any office.

If you've been challenged to find meaning in your life, you can ask yourself questions such as: *What brings me the greatest satisfaction to do? What do I feel drawn to, even though it may not make much logical sense? If my life were over tomorrow, what would I have regretted not doing?*

It doesn't matter where or how you find meaning—in creating music that will never make money but soothes the heart of everyone who listens, as one friend does, or making a peaceful home for her children, as another does, or by helping preserve the environment, or yes, through the work you get paid to do. What's important is that your soul answers yes.

30

Expand Your Notion of Love

"We are put on earth for a little space, that
we may learn to bear the beams of love."

—*William Blake*

Like the better-known Mother Teresa, Dorothy Day was
a Catholic who took the message to love thy neighbor
to heart. Along with Peter Maurin, a former priest, she
founded the Catholic Worker movement in 1933, a series
of communities around the United States dedicated to
"voluntary poverty, prayer, and hospitality for the homeless, exiled, hungry and forsaken," as the website puts it.
Twenty-four years after her death, over 185 communities, which she called Houses of Hospitality, carry on
her work, and there is a movement within the Catholic
Church to make her a saint. In her autobiography *The
Long Loneliness,* Dorothy wrote, "We have all known the
long loneliness and we have learned that the only solution
is love and that love comes with community."

When we think about creating happiness, we can't help
but consider love. Here's how another famous Catholic,
Thomas Merton, put it: "A happiness that is sought for
ourselves alone can never be found... True happiness is
found in unselfish love, a love that increases in proportion
as it is shared."

In this culture, when we think of love, we tend to conceive of it only in romantic terms, the love for the one and only soul mate we all search for, some of us successfully, others not. And it is true that this kind of love creates happiness: Study after study has shown that married folks tend to be happier than single ones. But equating happiness only with romantic love narrows it unnecessarily for everyone, not just those without a partner.

The great philosopher Aristotle, for instance, believed that the happy life was to be found in creating genuine friendships, in forging lasting bonds to others that were not contingent upon romance. Perhaps Aristotle was on to something—when asked what you need to be happy, most people first mention close relationships. And when the Gallup organization looked at 198,000 factors to find which distinguish more profitable and productive companies from average ones, one of the top ten was whether people had a best friend at work!

As these facts demonstrate, no matter our particular romantic circumstances, we are all here to love, to open our hearts to the majesty and mystery of the human capacity to care for and about other beings. Restricting it mentally to one particular form means we miss out on dozens of ways we could find every day to be happy. Caring for an aging mother, as my friend Ann does, being ready to leap to neighbors' help with food and friendly words, like my friend Graceanna, raising six vibrant, mentally and emotionally healthy children like my friend Molly, feeding the homeless like Dorothy Day—the love that is created through these heartfelt expressions is no less important or meaningful than romantic love.

When it comes to love, the question is not whether, but how and where. *How wide can my heart open? How can I be kinder, more patient with those I encounter? How can I not take my family members for granted? How can I allow myself to experience even more deeply the love of others? Where is there someone in need of my smile, my touch, my encouraging word? Where does the river of love want to flow now in me?*

In loving and being loved, we become most truly ourselves. Through this experience and expression of our essence, we create a sense of true joy. Here's how Daphne Rose Kingma puts it: "No matter what we do, say, accomplish, or become, it is our capacity to love that ultimately defines us. In the end, nothing we do or say in this lifetime will matter as much as the ways we have loved one another."

31

Revel in Life's Simple Pleasures

"It is not how much we have, but how much we enjoy that makes happiness."

—*Charles Spurgeon*

I love this quote, because I've been spending a lot of time wondering how I can enjoy the moments of my life more. But it has special meaning because of how it came to me. I was doing a signing for *Trusting Yourself.* I always ask folks to share what brings them to these events. A woman in the audience I'll call Lisa said, "I'm here because my husband is dying, I have two teenagers who are acting out, I've been a stay-at-home mom and I need to somehow support my family after my husband's death. I need to learn to trust myself." My heart went out to her. Later she sent me a thank-you card with the Spurgeon quote, which really affected me—despite all that she is dealing with, she took time out not only to thank me but to pick a card on *enjoyment.*

Lisa knows the secret that Spurgeon refers to—that even in times of sorrow or challenge or just in the midst of an ordinary day, we can take time for the things that give us pleasure. In fact, we need to, for they help make life worth living and replenish us for whatever we must do that is not so wonderful. Simple pleasures are little ordinary activities or indulgences that won't break the bank and give us energy, peace, or joy. Lisa's list includes walking every morning with her friend, reading, and painting her kitchen.

Every one of us has a different list. I once edited a book called *Simple Pleasures,* which really helped me understand how different we all are when it comes to the things that create enjoyment. One person's Chunky Monkey ice cream is another person's piano playing. I love getting into water of any kind—warm pools, hot tubs, showers. I love dancing and lying down.

What's your list? What are the things that bring a song to your heart, that make you go *Ahhhh, it's good to be alive?* These small things give big payoffs. Edward Diener, a University of Illinois researcher specializing in happiness, has discovered that "Happiness is how frequently you're happy, not how intensely."

Simple pleasures, indulged in frequently, are a key way to feel happy often. You can do them for no reason at all, or use them, as author Alexandra Stoddard does, as carrots, rewards for doing something unpleasant or challenging.

This is not permission to eat a dozen donuts or drink seven margaritas at one sitting. Such actions may bring momentary pleasure, but the consequences are not pretty. I'm suggesting you consider those things that bring enjoyment with no bad aftertaste. And the more we savor the experience—really tasting the one ounce of chocolate, for instance—the more we will enjoy without overindulging.

What this asks of us is to really take in the experience of enjoyment—fully feel, taste, smell, hear, see—so that we get the full measure of pleasure. The more we get receptive to our own experience, the greater our sense of happiness will be.

There is some research that indicates people can habituate to pleasure, so that they constantly need to up the ante. So instead of a simple hot bath, suddenly it must be in a Grecian spa with attractive attendants fanning you as you lie there. That's not my experience. If you truly soak the enjoyment in, certain pleasures are enduring.

Whether you have a few old favorites or find yourself going for something new, don't neglect this path to happiness. Lest you think it's self-indulgent, consider this passage from the Talmud: "Everyone will be called to account for all the legitimate pleasures which he or she has failed to enjoy."

32

Find Ways to
Enjoy Your Work

"I never did day's work in my life. It was all fun."
—*Thomas Edison*

One day, years ago, a person was driving toward a toll-booth at the San Francisco Bay Bridge. In a widely circulated, anonymous story, the person wrote: "I heard loud music... I looked at the tollbooth. Inside it, the man was dancing. 'What are you doing?' I asked. 'I'm having a party,' he said. 'What about the rest of these people?' I looked over at other booths; nothing moving there.

"'Vertical coffins,'" the toll taker replied. "'At 8:30 every morning, live people get in. Then they die for eight hours. At 4:30, like Lazarus from the dead, they reemerge and go home. For eight hours, brain is on hold, dead on the job. Going through the motions...

"'I'm going to be a dancer someday.' He pointed to the administration building. 'My bosses are in there, and they're paying for my training... I don't understand why anybody would think my job is boring. I have a corner office, glass on all sides. I can see the Golden Gate, San Francisco, the Berkeley hills; half the Western world vacations here and I just stroll in every day and practice dancing.'"

Work, the daily grind. We spend more waking hours at our jobs than in our homes. And as economic conditions tighten, those who are working feel the need to work more just to ensure a place at the employment table. According to the International Labour Organization, the average American now works 1,979 hours per year—over 400 hours more than Europeans and over 100 more than the Japanese, an increase in the last two decades of a full week per year. In a survey by the National Sleep Foundation, 38 percent of respondents say they work more than 50 hours a week, with professionals and managers clocking vastly more. And leisure is not on our minds: When asked in a RoperASW survey in 2003 whether they would prefer more money or more time off, only 27 percent of people polled picked the time.

Since we spend so much time there, how can we enjoy what we're doing as much as possible? It's a relatively easy question to answer for those who find meaning through work and have the chance to use their strengths in the workplace. But on average in organizations, research shows, less than one third of us have that privilege.

There is another way. In the monastic writings of both Eastern and Western traditions, we are reminded that like the toll taker, it is possible to find happiness in any task, from dog training to dishwashing. "Whether or not our work is dehumanizing depends on how we approach it," write the Monks of New Skete, an Eastern Orthodox community in upstate New York. "If we endure our work as a necessary evil at best, if we spend a third of our adult lives at this, then how can we not expect our life to be alienated, fragmented, unhappy... [U]nless we wish to allow the work we hate to crush our psyche and spirit, we're going to have to face the fact that we have to find a positive way to view it, to make it work out for us." Spiritual teacher Meister Eckhart says what is needed is "Doing the next thing you have to do, doing it with your whole heart, and finding delight in doing it."

But how to do it wholeheartedly? Each of us has to find our own answer to that question. Sometimes our lack of ability to enjoy work is a clue that we are so ill-suited to it that we must find something, anything, else to do. I spent a year as a teacher's helper in a kindergarten class of severely handicapped kids. I was miserable every day; I much preferred being a cashier at minimum wage.

Often, however, we can find ways to enjoy our work, no matter what it is. One that is suggested by spiritual teachers is to pay close attention to the task, to infuse it with great awareness—to really feel your fingers on the keyboard, to notice the rag as you wipe it across the table, to focus totally on the person who is making a request of you. With this singularity of attention, we become wholehearted. There's no part of us wishing to be anywhere else; we're just in this very moment, doing this very thing.

Another is to engage in whatever you're doing in the spirit of service. A recent study of hospital cleaners found that many of them considered their work challenging, respected, and critical to the health of patients. Like these cleaners, you can enjoy work more when you recognize that cooking, meeting with your team, driving a truck—whatever it is that you do for work—contributes to the well-being of other human beings and allows you to cultivate the qualities of the heart—patience, kindness, courage, generosity. From this place, it is possible to use work as a vehicle for spiritual and emotional growth. Or see it, like the toll taker, as a step on the way toward something else, a training that will better prepare us for what you'd prefer to do, and look for a way to make it fun.

Yet another way is to revel in the fact of accomplishment itself—that the report is complete, the kids put to bed, the deal signed. There is a wonderful sense of satisfaction in a job well done that is not to be ignored. That's why I've always loved the story of Creation, when God looks upon what He has done and proclaims it good. If God can take pride and enjoyment in His work, why shouldn't we?

33

Lose Yourself in Something

*"In every part and corner of our life,
to lose oneself is to be a gainer,
to forget oneself is to be happy."*
—*Robert Louis Stevenson*

Dave is a backcountry skier. He's now standing at the top of a mountain in Utah, which he's spent the last three hours climbing, and is about to reap the bounty: three thousand vertical feet of waist-deep powder, a crisp bluebird morning, and no one but his partner and a pair of soaring golden eagles in sight. The only thing on his mind is the blast of cold champagne snow billowing around his face as he links turn after turn down the steep wall. Finally he's standing at the bottom, panting, quivering, and hooting with admiration at the arcs he's just painted down this pristine canvas. Dave is more fully alive at this moment than he's ever been.

Mihaly Csikszentmihalyi, professor of social science at the Peter Drucker School of Business at Claremont University, was the first to identify the particular form of happiness Dave experienced. He called it flow, a state of mind when we are performing at our best, are involved fully in a task, and enjoy ourselves most. The poet David

Whyte calls it the "numinous experience of the present where we forget ourselves in the consummation of the moment."

This self-forgetfulness is at the heart of flow, whether it is expressed through writing a poem or racing down a mountain trail on a bike. Because we forget ourselves, flow is usually experienced as an absence of emotion; you tend to feel nothing at the time because you are fully absorbed in the task.

Having studied the phenomenon for decades, Csikszentmihalyi notes that no matter whether you experience it from a mental or physical task, flow is created under certain specific conditions: You are doing something challenging that requires competency and has a clear goal; you concentrate on it; you simultaneously have a sense of control and effortless involvement; your sense of self vanishes; and time stops. Flow, they've discovered, is most likely to occur when we are neither bored nor anxious and when we are using our particular strengths on behalf of something that is challenging but not impossible. When you experience flow, what matters is the process of doing itself, rather than any potential rewards. Because flow requires the full engagement of our capacities, it creates deep gratification.

Csikszentmihalyi and his colleagues have studied thousands of people and collected millions of samples of flow (by randomly beeping subjects throughout the day and finding out how engaged they are). What they've discovered is that some folks experience flow often; others not at all. Those who do experience flow consider themselves happier and more optimistic than others. Those who don't tend not to challenge themselves in any way—they hang out at malls more, watch TV more. They have more leisure time, but don't know what to do with it; they often feel bored and unhappy.

In one study by colleagues of Csikszentmihalyi, reported by David G. Myers in *The Pursuit of Happiness*, "3 percent of those who are watching TV experience flow, 39 percent report feeling apathetic. For those engaged in arts and hobbies the percentages flip-flop: 47 percent report flow and 4 percent report apathy. In fact, the *less* expensive (and generally more involving) a leisure activity, the *happier* people are while doing it. Most people are happier gardening than power boating, talking to friends than watching TV... Well-being resides not in mindless passivity but in mindful challenges."

Are you a bored couch potato? What could you do that could increase the possibility of experiencing flow? Learning photography? Gardening? Writing a book? One way to get started is to write down three times you've felt most alive. What were you doing? How could you do that more? The more we challenge ourselves—mentally, physically, emotionally—the greater a sense of gratification we will experience.

34

Make Your Peace
with Money

"Money never made a man happy yet, nor
will it... Instead of its filling a vacuum, it
makes one. If it satisfies one want, it doubles
and trebles that want another way."

—*Benjamin Franklin*

"It is a kind of spiritual snobbery that makes
people think they can be happy without money."

—*Albert Camus*

For six months a year for the past three years—forever in
my daughter Ana's life—I have worked not only during the
week with clients, but virtually every weekend as I write a
new book. (I recover and play with my family on the weekends in the other six months.) Yesterday she asked me why
I had to write. "Well," I said, "I love to think about these
things and to hopefully help myself and others be happier.
And I also do it so that we can pay for this house and your
school and the pool and all the other things we have."

"Do you *have* to?" she pleaded. I thought seriously
about her question.

"No," I replied. "We could live somewhere smaller, in a less-expensive state, send you to a public school, and have no pool."

"But I want this house and my school and the pool—and Mama too!" she wailed.

How human! Like Franklin says in the opening quote, the more we have, the more we tend to want. I read recently that when John D. Rockefeller, the richest man of his times, was asked what would make him happy, he retorted, "One dollar more."

A fascinating study reveals how common Rockefeller's response is. People of various income levels were asked how much more money they needed to be happy. Individuals making $20,000 thought $30,000 would do it. People who made $45,000 thought the magic number was $60,000, while people at $100,000 were convinced that if only they made $200,000, they would finally be happy. In another study, people were asked in 1957 if they had what they needed to be happy. Thirty percent said yes. The study was repeated in 1992, and again only 30 percent of folks answered in the affirmative, despite the fact that the standard of living had risen dramatically over those decades. And researchers say that study after study shows that the desire for material goods, which has gone hand in hand with the rise in income in the West, is actually a happiness suppressant.

Yet as anyone who has been extremely poor will tell you, Camus is right too. We all need the basics of food, shelter, and health care, and without them our lives can be pretty bleak. That's why when people around the world are asked if they are satisfied with their lives over-all, folks in the affluent countries of North America and Western Europe score highest. Their lives are materially easier. Interestingly, however, when the same people are asked if they are happy in this moment, Nigeria, a country of extreme poverty, ranks highest, followed by Mexico, Venezuela, El Salvador, Puerto Rico, Vietnam, and Cambodia, proving once again that the relationship between happiness and money is not as straightforward as one might imagine.

The best way I've learned to think about it comes from a book I once read in which the author said money is like oxygen. Just like oxygen, its lack can cause serious problems, but once your body has what it needs, its abundance is irrelevant. It's when you try to define need that you can get into money trouble. That's why I took Ana's question so seriously. No, we don't *need* a lot of the things I work for; we could survive without them. So am I sacrificing my family's happiness to provide a whole lot of stuff? If I didn't enjoy what I do, if it didn't bring a sense of purpose to my life, if I were doing it only for the money, I would seriously consider stopping writing and change my financial life accordingly.

Financial guru Suze Orman says that "happiness is not tied to how much money you have—how much you had in the past or hope to have in the future—but how you deal with what you have right now." It's hard to be happy, she points out, when your credit card debt is $9,205, the current average for U.S. families, according to *CardWeb. com*. Getting out of debt will create happiness far greater, she claims, than the fancy dinner, wide-screen TV, or vacations you forgo to put your financial house in order.

As an entrepreneur, I've experienced wild fluctuations in income in the thirty years or so I've been working, and I agree wholeheartedly with Suze—happiness is living within my means. In the lean times, what made me miserable was not so much the reductions when they came, but the debt that piled up until I changed my lifestyle. Two hundred years ago, Charles Dickens, who knew of what he spoke, said, "Annual income twenty pounds, annual expenditure nineteen six, result happiness. Annual income twenty pounds, annual expenditure twenty pounds ought and six, result misery."

If debt is standing in the way of your being happy, get financial help. And be willing to make a bold move. Friends of mine are selling their house and moving their family into a condo so that they can reduce their overhead. My tenants are leaving California to go to a state where they can afford to buy a home. These sacrifices don't hurt so much when we do them on behalf of a truly happier life.

Money may not buy us happiness, but debt makes us miserable for sure. One way to live within our means and recognize that we have enough is to differentiate between needs and wants. I may want a red Beetle convertible, but I certainly don't need one; my old car still runs. When I appreciate what I do have—a functional car and no car loan—I can be happy with what I have rather than longing for what I do not.

35

Realize We Aren't Meant to Be Happy All the Time

"When you are unhappy, is there anything
more maddening than to be told that you
should be contented with your lot?"

—*Kathleen Norris*

I was flipping through a catalog. My eyes were drawn to a large plaque that you could buy to put over your couch. In large letters it read: IT'S ALL GOOD.

My blood began to boil. *It's not all good!* There is tremendous suffering in the world. So many of us have to bear the burden of so much. There are bombings and starvation, layoffs and abuse, intractable poverty and senseless violence. I recently learned that kids as young as twelve are cutting themselves all over their bodies to create scars in what's described as the latest teenage fad. Just yesterday I heard of two young women whose mother and father are both in the hospital with terminal cancer.

To experience happiness in our daily lives does not mean hiding our heads in the sand. It's not about feeling absolutely wonderful all the livelong day. We're meant to feel bad as well as good—the part of our brains that experiences fear, worry, sorrow, and anger is there to protect us from danger and spur us into action. When a speeding car is bearing down on you, it's not too smart to think, "Isn't that good?" Rather, you feel fear and get the hell out of the way.

What being happy is about, I believe, is having a home base of contentment and well-being that you return to when the immediate crisis is over, rather than being stuck in chronic anger, worry, or fear. It's about noticing what you can enjoy and appreciate about the rest of your life even as you face your challenges. It's about feeling empowered to take actions that hopefully will improve the situation and enjoying yourself along the way. It's about creating the maximum possibilities for meaning or joy in the midst of the terrible thing.

So many of us hold ourselves back from the happiness we could experience moment to moment because we think it means we have to be in denial of our own pain or that of the world. That's just not true. Unhappiness is often an important signal for change of some sort. That's why it's right not to feel happy all the time. But once you get the message, you've got a choice—to keep focusing on the misery or to take the actions you can to increase contentment and well-being in yourself and others.

That's what the two sisters did. Both were engaged to be married, and when they found out that their parents were dying, they decided to hold a double wedding at the hospital so their mom and dad could attend. The nurses helped decorate the floor in a wedding motif and the ceremony was full of tears of joy as well as sorrow.

This is spiritual courage—the willingness to choose to be happy in the face of grief or anger without denying or repressing our painful feelings. It's what Alfred Adler meant when he said, "There is a courage of happiness as well as a courage of sorrow." You shouldn't feel happy all the time—but are you courageous enough to feel as happy as you can?

36

Remember, You Always Have Choices

> "If you choose not to decide—
> you still have made a choice!"
>
> —*Neil Peart*

Martha was complaining to me that she was unhappy because she had "had" to follow her husband around the country from job to job for the past twenty years. I asked, "Did he tie you up and throw you into the car? Did he lock you in the house so you couldn't escape? You chose to go—every single time, you made a choice to stay in your relationship rather than go off on your own."

It took her a long time to believe that the choice had been hers each time. But finally she got the point when

I asked her the following question: "How would your belief about this change if you looked at your decisions as a choice for love rather than something that happened against your will?"

"Well," she replied, "I guess I would have been happier along the way."

Until that moment, Martha was wedded to feeling like a victim of her circumstances, and people who feel like victims are rarely happy. Believing themselves to be mere pawns in the game of life, they pay attention only to the limitations and hardships of any given situation and feel wretched and despairing.

The truth is we always have choices, if only to choose the meaning we make out of the circumstances we find ourselves in. And the more we experience our freedom of choice, the happier our lives are.

The person who has written most profoundly on this topic is Viktor Frankl. For five years Frankl was imprisoned in Auschwitz and other concentration camps. He noticed that those who survived were not necessarily stronger than others, but those who experienced an inner freedom of thought—recognizing that the Nazis could control their bodies, but not their minds. In one of the book's most famous passages, he wrote, "Everything can be taken from a man but the last of human freedoms, the right to choose one's attitude in any given set of circumstances—the right to choose one's own way."

Most of us reading this book are not in such extreme circumstances, and thus our options are much greater. Yet we go around thinking all the time, I don't have any choice.

Of course we do—we just don't want it badly enough to pay the price or haven't thought creatively enough about how to get it. That's why the ancient Greek philosopher Thucydides proclaimed that "the secret of Happiness is Freedom, and the secret of Freedom, Courage." If we want to be truly happy, we must take responsibility for our lives and the choices we make (or choose not to make). And that takes courage—the courage to be ourselves.

Something to consider as you ponder the choices available to you: Many physicists believe that the future is actually formed by the choices we make. Here's how futurist John Schaar describes it: "The future is not a result of choices among alternative paths offered by the present, but a place that is created—created first in the mind and will, created next in activity. The future is not some place we are going to, but one we are creating. The paths are not to be found, but made, and the activity of making them, changes both the maker and the destination."

When Martha realized that she'd been choosing for love all this time, she decided that she might as well enjoy her choice. She began to think of her relationship as her life's masterpiece. She began to be nicer to her husband, which of course made him nicer to her in return. She realized that she loved making beautiful environments for the two of them to nest in and moving around a lot enabled her to exercise that passion often. She became happier—right in the midst of the situation she previously considered unbearable.

The happiness we thought elusive is right under our noses when we recognize that we do not have to be victims of our circumstances.

37

Do You Need a Nice REST?

"Life catches up with you sometimes."
—*Gary McDarby*

Four times this week, when I've asked people how they feel, they have responded with some version of: "I'm feeling a bit lowly. I think I'm tired." My friend Graceanna, usually the queen of cheer, proclaimed, "I'm exhausted. Even though it's only six p.m., as soon as we've finished talking, I am going to crawl into bed with some trashy magazines and stay in there till morning."

Smart woman. Rather than assuming that what she was feeling was depression, she understands that it's hard to be happy when you're worn out and took immediate steps to rectify the situation.

This is no small feat. With all the demands on our attention, it's extremely difficult to tune out the world. But I do believe that's one of the reasons we're not as happy as we would like to be. Our systems get depleted—mentally, emotionally, spiritually, and physically—and rather than turn inward and rejuvenate, we caffeinate, we push through, we trudge—and I do mean trudge—on. We're running on empty and wondering why life feels so bleak. In a study of citizens of L.A. County, those who slept less than seven hours per night were twice as likely to be depressed as those who got adequate shut-eye. The head of the Stanford Sleep Disorders Center, William Dement, says, "The national sleep debt is larger and more important than the national monetary debt."

But it's not just more sleep we need. It's tuning the world out so that we can tune ourselves in. It's *idleness,* to use a word that would seem in this day and age to be worse than any swearword. We are bombarded with constant stimulation, demands to put attention everywhere but on ourselves. I was recently at the Chicago airport trying to have lunch in the only available spot—a sports bar. It had at least twenty-five TVs going and various neon ticker tapes were giving other scores. On top of that there was pop music blaring, and people were yelling at one another in an attempt to converse.

The notion that tuning out the world might be a way to feel happier is quite foreign. And yet, in Japan it is common for those suffering from depression or anxiety to do "quiet therapy," a combination of a week of bed rest and meditation. David Myers cites research by Peter Suedfeld at the University of British Columbia on REST: Restricted Environmental Stimulation Therapy. Suedfeld "offered hundreds of people a chance to tune more deeply into themselves through a literal day of REST, during which they would do nothing but lie quietly on a comfortable bed in the isolation of a dark, soundproof room. Food, water, and a chemical toilet were available, and communication was possible over an intercom." Guess what? They not only felt better but were able to make life changes such as stopping smoking or overcoming fears more easily.

I've been practicing my own form of REST for years. Whenever life gets too gray and my butt is dragging, I spend a whole day in bed. I sleep late, read trashy novels, and stare out the window, getting up only to make forays to the fridge or the bathroom. By the next day, I'm ready to engage wholeheartedly with life again.

Is a REST cure what you need to put the sparkle back into your psyche? It doesn't have to be a day in bed. Some folks find the same rejuvenation in nature. Or on a ski slope on a weekday. All that matters is that you have a chance to shut out the world and cocoon for a while. Where do you do your best hibernation? Is it time to make the world go away?

38

Expand Your
Happiness Portfolio

*"Just as a cautious businessman
avoids investing all his capital in one
concern, so wisdom would probably
admonish us also not to anticipate all our
happiness from one quarter alone."*
—*Sigmund Freud*

As a child, I was either in school or reading novels. Then I
fell in love and that was so incredible that love became my
happiness be-all and end-all. When the man was around,
the sun shone in my heart. When he was gone, I plunged
into darkness. *Aha,* I reasoned, *find a man who is always
around and you'll be eternally happy.* It took me several
rounds to discover that no man is always there and that
even if he were glued to my side, having all my happiness eggs in one basket was dangerous indeed. I returned
to reading.

Years ago, hearing of my fate, a friend taught me to do
needlepoint so I could have at least one alternative. After
creating large numbers of pillows that still grace the houses
of friends and family, I got arthritis in my hands and had
to give it up. But I've continued to expand my happiness

repertoire to include cooking, leading workshops, giving speeches, writing books, learning all I can about the qualities of the heart.

Expanding my repertoire was important for the same reasons a diversified portfolio is. It spreads the risk. When I thought my happiness could be found only with the man in my life, I spent all my time worrying about losing him—after all, how could I possibly survive if something happened to him? I fantasized car wrecks, plane crashes, heart attacks. I never actually spent any time being happy because I spent all my time worrying about losing my happiness source.

It was only when I began to experience satisfaction and fulfillment from a number of places—work, love, friendship—that I came to see that the source of my happiness was my own engagement with life, with the persons, places, and things that give my existence pleasure and meaning. And the more I cultivate, the happier my life is because I'm not dependent on any one as the sole source.

Research bears this out. Studies show that women tend to do better than men when a spouse dies, because men tend to put all their relationship energy into their marriage, while women diversify with other strong relationships that give them other happiness outlets to fall back on.

What does your happiness portfolio look like? What gives you satisfaction and pleasure? What brings you a sense of fulfillment? Is there some aspect of happiness as described in Chapter 2 that you want to cultivate? Is life asking you to expand your repertoire?

Since change is inevitable, what has worked in the past may no longer be available or give the sense of satisfaction it once did. When that happens, you have a choice—to bemoan your fate or find something else. My father was a small-town doctor who derived 100 percent of his happiness from work. When he retired, I was afraid he would melt into misery. But he found new happiness outlets—he became a philosophy instructor, learned to bake bread and vacuum the house, worked more in his garden.

I have a friend who has always derived happiness from physical activity—windsurfing, skiing, martial arts. Now, in his late fifties, the condition of his body is requiring him to find alternatives. He took up yoga, but even that is proving too difficult for his knees and shoulders. He could get resentful. Or he could, as he has, use the situation to expand his happiness portfolio by asking himself what pleasures can be found in the slower, gentler pace that is being required of him.

Like a diamond, happiness has many sides, but its brilliance is more than the sum of its parts. Taken individually, each way to happiness has something to contribute to our sense of well-being. Taken together, our lives begin to have that sparkle and shine that we call joy. Expand your happiness portfolio. It's the most valuable one you have.

39

Practice Gratefulness

"In our daily lives, we must see that it is
not happiness that makes us grateful but
gratefulness that makes us happy."

—*Anonymous*

Writing books on virtues as I have done, I live in fear of being seen as a hypocrite. That's why I am careful to say that I don't consider myself kinder, more grateful, generous, patient, or self-trusting than others. I just read and think about these things a lot and practice what I've learned. Emphasis on the word "practice."

That's why I can say that I know for sure that one of the greatest ways to be happier is to be more grateful. I've been diligently practicing that one for about ten years now, ever since my first book on gratitude, *The Grateful Heart,* and I got a boost in my learning a few years later with *Attitudes of Gratitude.* Truly nothing that I have done before or since has had such an effect on my level of daily happiness.

It's so simple, really. The more we give thanks for what we have, the more aware we are of what we have to be happy about and the happier we feel. There's an old Irish proverb that expresses this perfectly: "Count your joys instead of your woes. Count your friends instead of your foes." Neuroscientists now know why being grateful feels good. Every time we appreciate something, we flood our bodies with endorphins, which produce a sense of well-being.

The practice of gratitude is simple, but for some of us it's not so easy. Recently I had a client, Rose, who, when I suggested that she try counting her blessings, responded, "I tried that gratitude thing once. But every time I began to give thanks, all the terrible things in the world and in my life came flooding into my mind. It felt phony to be appreciative when so much of my life is so awful."

I explained that I didn't believe being thankful was about denying what was difficult. Rather, because those things get so much of our mental air space, counting our blessings was a chance to notice what was also present but not necessarily on our radar screen—namely, the good in our lives. I encouraged her to take two minutes at the end of the day for one week to be grateful and notice the effect. Rose called the following week. "I did it," she exclaimed. "I do have things to be thankful for, even in the midst of my troubles. And do you know what? I don't feel as depressed as usual."

Don't take Rose's word for it. Try it yourself. Make it easy to do or else you won't remember. In my family, we do it at the dinner table because we usually eat together. The three of us plus any guests go around and say one thing we are thankful for that day. Before Ana could talk, she would point her little finger at Don and me. You'll be amazed at how loving and connected you'll feel toward those around you and how much brighter your life will seem. Do it first thing in the morning. Do it when you're driving home from work. There's no wrong way.

Besides my evening ritual, I do it when I find myself worrying about the people or circumstances of my life. Worry is always about the future and counting our blessings brings us into this present moment. So when my mind turns to all that could go wrong, I think, *Yes, but in this moment, my family is healthy, we have a roof over our heads, Don and I have jobs.* Instantly my mood lightens.

It's the nature of desire to always want something more or different. Being thankful is the best way I know to get off the wheel of craving. Here's how G. K. Chesterton put it one hundred years ago: "I would maintain that thanks are the highest form of thought, and that gratitude is happiness doubled by wonder." Double your happiness—count your blessings and your spirits will soar.

40

Get Out of Yourself

> "Lock your house, go across the
> railroad tracks and find someone in
> need and do something for him."
>
> —*Karl Menninger's advice to a man who said he*
> *was going to have a nervous breakdown*

Cynthia was going through a painful divorce that she initiated. I'd helped her figure out what she wanted to do and how to go about doing it. One reason she'd decided on divorce was that she hadn't been happy for many years. As the process went on, she felt more and more that she was doing the right thing. But she still wasn't happy. "All I do is feel sorry for myself," she said one day. "Sorry that my marriage didn't work out, that I'm living in this tiny apartment, that my soon-to-be ex doesn't understand why it's necessary to do this. I'm tired of focusing only on me."

"Well," I responded, "it's important to feel your feelings of grief, anger, and disappointment. But it's been a while now. I think you're on to something when you say you're sick of being self-absorbed." I gave her an assignment to do something nice for someone else at least once a day for the next week. And sure enough, when we talked next, she was feeling more upbeat than she had in years.

When we have difficulties in our lives, it's easy to become self-involved. And at times, it's quite appropriate—we may need to turn inward to heal and regroup. But if you find yourself marooned there, you can spiral downward into a darker and darker gloom where the world narrows down to only your problem. That's why the visionary psychiatrist Karl Menninger gave the advice he did in the opening quote. He wanted his client to get out of himself.

Psychologist Bernard Rimland conducted an experiment in which he asked 216 students to think of the ten people they knew best. Then he asked them to rate each person as happy or not. Then as selfish or not. What he discovered about these 2,160 people is that 70 percent of those who seemed happy were rated as unselfish, whereas 95 percent of selfish folks were rated unhappy. Wrote Rimland in response, "Selfish people are, by definition, those whose activities are devoted to *bringing themselves happiness*. Yet, at least as judged by others, these selfish people are far less likely to be happy than those whose efforts are devoted to making others happy."

Oftentimes we're told that the reason helping others makes us happier is because when we compare our lives to others in need, we wake up to the fact that we don't have it so bad. But recent breakthroughs in neuroscience indicate other positive benefits for getting out of ourselves. When we act generously toward others, our left prefrontal lobe of our neocortex gets activated, which stimulates feelings of happiness; our bodies are flooded with feel-good hormones, and our immune function as measured by the number of T cells increases. In other words, acting good to someone else makes us feel good inside.

And don't think your life is too awful or you are too miserable to benefit. Getting out of yourself is a powerful happiness creator, no matter your circumstances. Author Jackie Waldman, who has multiple sclerosis, noticed that her disease was less troublesome the more she volunteered. She wondered if that was true for others with serious physical, mental, or emotional difficulties and ended up writing a series of books on the phenomenon, beginning with *The Courage to Give.*

When we focus on others, we shower ourselves with good feelings, too.

41

Accept the Duty of Delight

"Life is not meant to be easy, my child;
but take courage—it can be delightful."
—*George Bernard Shaw*

A friend had a beloved pet die. Suddenly she became afraid of all the potential losses in her life—what if her son was killed? Her husband? What if her house burned down? What if she lost her job?

There are no guarantees against tragedy striking. But what we can do when we start down this fearful path is to take the opportunity to appreciate that what we are afraid of losing is right in front of us. We can't control the future, but we can truly enjoy the person, place, or thing right now and we can experience the maximum joy possible in this very moment.

Indeed, it is precisely because life is unpredictable that we have the "duty of delight," as Dorothy Day, founder of the Catholic Worker movement, called it, a responsibility to relish, cherish, and value the gifts we have been given so that when they are taken away—through death or other changes that life's impermanence brings our way—we will not have to also bear the pain of having failed to appreciate what we had. My friend Charon learned this the hard way: "When my sister was killed in an automobile accident, after a time of grieving, it became clear to me that the best way to honor her memory was to celebrate all of life's gifts and not take anyone or anything for granted again."

This appreciation is the greatest antidote to fear of loss that I have discovered in my life. Every time I find myself worrying about someone or something I love, I stop and take it as a signal to truly feel my joy at having received such wonderful gifts: the slant of light in my house, Don's gentle presence, Ana's bright spirit.

I've done a lot of airplane travel in the past five years, and since 9/11, the reality of impermanence has been hard to ignore. I even flew the first day planes were in the air again, and let me tell you, that was terrifying. Now each time I kiss my husband and daughter goodbye, even just to see them off for the day, I am aware that it might be the last time. So I try to never waste the moment. I make sure I really feel the softness of Ana's cheek, really feel my husband's arms around me. I make sure I say "I love you," and feel their love for me. I don't want to miss any of the precious moments to love one another that have been granted to us. As a consequence, I have experienced more moments of delight in the past five years than in the previous four decades.

One wonderful way to practice the duty of delight is through what Thich Nhat Hanh calls "hugging meditation." I have done this at weddings and at workshops and speeches, as well as at my own front door. All you need is someone you care about. He or she doesn't even have to know what you are doing. You just do three hugs in silence. During the first hug, you remember that the person you are hugging will not always be here, that he or she sometime will die. With the second hug you remember that you will not always be here, that someday you will die. And with the third hug you realize that you are here, right now, together in this moment that will never come again. I guarantee that you will treasure the preciousness of the moment and the one you love.

Samuel Taylor Coleridge once said, "The happiness of life is made up of minute fractions—the little, soon forgotten charities of a kiss or a smile, a kind look or heartfelt compliment." When we remember our duty to delight, we won't miss out on them.

42

Take a Hormonal Happiness Shower

"It is impossible to walk rapidly and be unhappy."
—*Dr. Howard Murphy*

I was giving a talk on *The Power of Patience* and discussing patience strategies. A woman raised her hand. "I take a book with me everywhere so whenever I encounter a line, I have something to do. Is that cheating?"

"Whatever works, honey," I replied.

When it comes to being more patient or happy, as far as I'm concerned, there's no such thing as cheating. It's not about doing it "right," it's about noticing what's effective. I believe any solution—spiritual, emotional, physical, practical—that enhances your sense of well-being and allows you to be more gracious with life's ups and downs and more loving to those you encounter is worth doing.

That's why, in this section on activating daily happiness, I must mention exercise. You've heard of the benefits in terms of weight control and life expectancy. But aerobic exercise has been shown over and over to be a great mood elevator. Over one hundred studies confirm that happiness and health and fitness are highly correlated. As we exercise, we oxygenate our brains, creating better brain function, and flood our bodies with a 500 percent increase in endorphin production—you know, the feel-good hormones. That's why every time you work out, you give yourself a hormonal happiness shower.

In his book *Baby Steps to Happiness,* John Q. Baucom describes it this way: "Best-selling author Covert Bailey suggests that if the benefits of exercise could be put into a pill it would be the most widely-prescribed form of medication in history. In fact, the pill is already available—it takes thirty minutes to swallow—it's called *exercise.*"

Now I'm not an exercise fanatic by any means. But it's hard for me to ignore all the data. So I've made a commitment to work out thirty minutes a day three times a week. I've stuck to it for about a year now (mostly). I do feel better—I have more energy; I don't have to work as hard at focusing on what's right. The secret to getting this couch potato in motion was to make it part of my routine. I found a circuit-training place right by my daughter's school. I just go there before picking her up.

When clients come to me to work on being happier, I always suggest exercise as part of their happiness regimen. Here are some of the factors they have found that make it possible:

1. Rewards: One guy I work with bribed himself with a sailboat if he stuck to it for a year;

2. Find something you love to do: dance, yoga, biking—if you love it, it's easier to stick to;

3. Get a buddy, someone to do it with for company and motivation;

4. Make it a priority: a busy executive found that when she tried for fifteen minutes a day, it wasn't important enough for her to do, but when she increased her goal to thirty, she did it.

5. Find a regular time.

6. Burn a $20 bill every time you don't keep your commitment to yourself.

Experiment to discover what works for you. But find a way to do it. You'll feel, as one former slacker-turned-triathlete confided to me, "infinitely happier."

43

Shine Where You Are

*"The only true happiness comes from
squandering ourselves for a purpose."*
—*William Cowper*

Tami works for UPS. She's happy most of the time and when I asked her about that, here's what she told me: "I've been a driver for a long time and at some point, I got bored with my job. I thought, is this all there is? I'm really an artist at heart and would love to paint. But I'm a single mom with two young kids and the pay and benefits with UPS are good. So it made no sense to leave, except that I wanted more creative expression from my work. Then it hit me—I could do my art and bring happiness to others while I work."

She began collecting inspirational quotes and wrote them on small pieces of paper, which she then illustrated. Now she hands them out to folks who seem to need an encouraging word whom she encounters throughout the day. "Some people give me an odd look, but most people look forward to getting a message," she says. "I spend part of every evening creating these pieces and have been much happier since I began."

Tami has a friend, Charon. Charon works for a large corporation, doing typical corporate work. She too has found a way to shine—she started a Happy Club, which consists of Charon e-mailing large numbers of people quotes to inspire and uplift them at the start of each week.

We all want to live lives of purpose. In fact, our souls require it, and our ongoing happiness depends on it. But not everyone can develop a cure for AIDS or work with the U.N. We want to make a difference, but aren't even sure what we have to contribute. Ordinary life seems to create so many demands on our time and energy. We feel trapped inside a glass box by the circumstances of our existence. We stare out, wishing to be of use, if only we could escape the box.

What Tami and Charon know is that no matter who you are, no matter your circumstances, you can create more meaning and, therefore, happiness. You don't need to read a tome on purpose or take a year off on a mountaintop. All you need to do is to figure out, to paraphrase

Frederick Buckner, where your deep gladness and the world's needs meet.

What do you love to do? Where can you offer what you love right in the dailiness of your life? Do you enjoy cooking and therefore could make extra food and give it to homeless people? Or sing on the subway on the way to work? What if you considered yourself a peacemaker whose assignment is your very own team?

You can bemoan your miserable life. Or you can find ways to shine just where you are. All it requires is the belief that you can and a bit of ingenuity. Recently Tami has begun to create sayings of her own. One of her designs is a rooster weather vane with the words, "What if there were a different way?" What if indeed?

44

Become a Good Finder

"Who has good news?
Who has something good to say?"
—*Award-winning teacher Hal Urban*
to all his students

Zig Ziglar is one of the most popular motivational speakers and authors in the United States. His is a rags-to-riches story of being the tenth child in a family of twelve during the Depression. His father died when he was five, but he later became one of the top salespeople in the country. In his book *See You at the Top,* he describes a study of one hundred very successful people who ranged in age from the twenties to the seventies. Coming from a diversity of backgrounds, they only had one thing in common. They were all "good finders," searching for the good "in other people—and every situation."

Hal Urban, who would go on to become an award-winning teacher at the high school and university levels, as well as a speaker on positive character traits, was a young educator when he first read those words. And, as he relates in his book *Positive Words, Powerful Results,* they changed his life. He realized that, like so many of us, he spent most of his time "moaning, whining, grumbling, complaining." He not only resolved to become a "good finder" himself, but to encourage it in all his students. He began asking the questions at the beginning of this essay at the start of every single class he taught. Students could contribute anything—something from the news or their own lives, or something they were thankful for (he called this perpetual good news), or something complimentary about a classmate.

"Over the years of doing this," he wrote, "we heard just about every bit of good news possible. Some were small things, some were huge things... This simple little ritual also had a buildup effect. Each day we added to the good news of the previous day, and so on. And each day my students increased their awareness of all the good news going on around them all the time."

The first time he did it, he was not aware of the impact it would have. But when he gave his final exam and asked the question, "What are three things you learned in this class that were of the most value to you?" virtually everyone wrote about the good news practice. And former students he runs into even twenty years later still comment on it as one of the most valuable lessons they ever learned in school.

We can take a lesson from Hal. This good finding is a powerful practice for happiness. As Dan Baker puts it in *What Happy People Know,* "I tell people to look for the good in life, not the best. The best doesn't always happen. But good, in one form or another, always does."

We can become good finders by asking, "Who has good news? Who has something good to share?" We can do it in the evening with family. We can do it on long family trips in the car. We can do it at the beginning of team meetings. The important thing is to find a specific time and place to do it so it becomes a natural habit. Then not only will we be increasing our own happiness, but also that of those around us!

45

Keep Frustrations
in Perspective

"A happy life consists in tranquility of mind."
—*Cicero*

Many years ago, Sylvia Boorstein, now a renowned
Buddhist teacher, was a harried mother with four children
under the age of five. To keep her equilibrium, she painted
a large banner on her kitchen wall: this too shall pass. And
of course it did. Her children are now grown and have kids
of their own, and the exhaustion and overwhelming stress
of those years are but a dim memory.

Whatever frustrations or difficulties you are now fac-
ing, chances are they become more bearable if you, like
Sylvia, put them into some kind of perspective. There are
many techniques for keeping things in perspective. If it's
something you know will change, focusing on the fact
that it will someday be over—your child out of the terrible
twos, you out of the supermarket line—helps. If it's something you can't be confident will change—a chronic illness,
say, or unemployment—the perspective that's needed is
seeing this challenge as only a part of your existence and
not all consuming. It also helps to remember that things
always change—if only your own capacity to respond to

the challenge—and therefore you will not always be in this exact spot.

Perspective is the number one practice for cultivating patience, and patience is a happiness activator. Patience creates happiness because it makes us more resilient to life and content in the face of challenges. It does this by offering three precious gifts: First, perseverance, the ability to stick to something even when we can't see the immediate reward. This helps us make our dreams come true, which creates great joy. Second, acceptance, the ability to take life as it comes and not to add our own resistance to the pain inherent in any difficulty. This helps us to be happy under any circumstance. And finally, equanimity, evenness of mind, even under stress. This enables us to not be devastated by the slings and arrows of outrageous fortune, but to cultivate a happiness that goes beyond circumstance. Patience gives us equilibrium.

The Dalai Lama talks about this factor in *The Art of Happiness:* "even in worldly terms, in terms of our enjoying a happy day-to-day existence, the greater the level of calmness of our mind, the greater our peace of mind... if you possess this inner quality, a calmness of mind, a degree of stability within, then even if you lack various external facilities that you would normally consider necessary for happiness, it is still possible to live a happy and joyful life."

The proverb "This too shall pass" is attributed to King Solomon, who was asked by a sultan to come up with a statement that is true under all circumstances. Abraham Lincoln is reputed to be the first to use it in the United States. He told the story of Solomon and commented,

"How chastening in the hour of pride! How consoling in the depth of affliction!"

How can you remember to console yourself with perspective during the day? Post a note on your computer? Paint a banner in your kitchen? Ask yourself if it will matter in ten years, or ten minutes? The more you practice perspective, the less you'll get knocked over by every little bump in your path.

46

Find Your Tribe

"There's no house like the house of belonging."
—*David Whyte*

Last Thursday I went to a monthly meeting of a book group at the Union City, California, Borders bookstore. I'd been there once before. The group is composed of about a dozen people of all ages, races, and backgrounds drawn together by the desire to read and talk about issues that matter to them. They talk about the book for an hour or so, then head to the café to drink tea and share their lives. They have been meeting for years, and it is clear that this impromptu group has become a community of connection and support to one another.

Humans weren't meant to be alone all the time. For millennia we lived in small communities, knowing intimately the ins and outs of one another's lives. But in the last one hundred years or so, we have become increasingly socially isolated. Nuclear families have gotten smaller and smaller. Many of us have left traditional religion, which used to provide social connection as well as spiritual sustenance, and because of dual careers, our neighborhoods are empty from early morning until late at night when we crawl into bed.

But the longing to be connected to others still lives in us. Perhaps that's why so very many of us are depressed—there has been a tenfold increase in depression in the past forty years that is unexplained by biology, ecology, or income. In fact, studies of African Americans and Hispanics in the United States, who generally have greater family and community ties, show that they have less depression than whites, even though their material circumstances tend to be worse. Maybe we're unhappy because we're lonely.

I'll never forget a woman I met a few years ago at a retreat I was helping facilitate. "Where is my tribe?" she wailed. "I've spent my whole life searching for people I can feel connected to." We all need a group to be part of, a place in the social world where we feel like we belong. In one research study, happiness increased 30 percent by greater community interaction.

It doesn't matter where the group is—in cyberspace, in your hometown, or scattered around the globe. It doesn't matter what the focus of getting together is—a love of dogs, or books, or changing the world. What matters is that you find a clan, a tribe, where you can share your joys and sorrows, your gifts and challenges, and be likewise supported in return. One place to look is at your interests. How can you join or create a group about something you love?

My tribe is an informal one—it's a group of friends who are knit together through me who share a love of books and personal growth. They rarely interact with one another, but every time I speak with one, she always asks about the others: How is Ann doing? What about Stephanie? Did Molly finish the book? And I do the same for all their friends. The result is an experience of community, despite our living all over the country.

We each need to experience the sense of belonging.

47

Make a List of What You Enjoy about Yourself

"Men go abroad to wonder at the height of the mountains, at the huge waves of the sea, at the long courses of the rivers, at the vast compass of the ocean, at the circular motion of the stars, and they pass by themselves without wondering."

—*St. Augustine*

I have a friend who once said to me, "I'm never lonely because I always enjoy the contents of my mind." Her comment amazed me not only because at the time the contents of my mind were mostly torturous, but also because I was amazed at anyone who could boldly state what she enjoyed about herself. We've all been so trained to look outside ourselves for answers and entertainment, and to focus on all our flaws, that it's hard to even conceive of actually noticing what we enjoy about ourselves. It seems a bit conceited, right? Or self-aggrandizing.

Then I came across a quote by Joseph Addison: "True happiness... arises, in the first place, from the enjoyment of one's self." I thought, *Of course. I spend more time with me than anyone else does, and if I don't enjoy myself, think of all the moments of potential happiness I am missing out on.* We spend endless hours torturing ourselves about our imperfections and failings, how about spending a few moments figuring out what brings us pleasure so that we can engage those resources whenever we want to?

This is not to say it's easy. When I work with clients, we always end by saying what we've appreciated about ourselves during the call. I've been doing it for a long time, and it still feels awkward. But self-appreciation and enjoyment are just a hop, skip, and a jump apart—you probably can't enjoy something you don't appreciate about yourself.

You're lucky—you don't have to share what you discover about yourself. You can keep it all to yourself and enjoy it anytime you want for an instant happiness experience. But in order to make this real, I'll go out on a limb and share my answer.

One thing I enjoy about myself is my capacity to take everything I've read and heard and store it in my head. Then it pops out when I need it. It happened just the other day—I was facilitating a meeting and feeling rather useless. Then something I read a year ago popped in and I presented it, which helped a lot in the moment. I got a double dose of happiness—I was happy that I recalled it and happy that it was useful.

Now it's your turn. Pick just one thing to start. How does it make you feel to think about it? Pretty happy, right? To get a hit of joy, you don't even have to do it—all you have to do is remember. In the mind, there is no difference. You'll get the lift from anticipating, from doing, and from remembering. Now that's a lot of enjoyment.

48

Do an Integrity Check

"Happiness is when what you think, what you say, and what you do are in harmony."
—*Mahatma Gandhi*

Born into poverty, married at barely fourteen, the mother of six children, and a grandmother at only twenty-nine, country-western star Loretta Lynn knew personally about the hard lives of blue-collar women. That's why, in the sixties and seventies, when she began to pen her own songs— as her children slept and she taught herself guitar from a correspondence course—she sang about the issues women struggle with: standing up for yourself, the heartbreak of infidelity, pregnancy. She so believed in her role as the voice for unheard women that she wrote about things that at the time were very controversial, particularly in the conservative country-western world.

The most notorious was "The Pill," a celebration of the sexual freedom finally afforded women by reliable birth control. Loretta was denounced from church pulpits and banned by many radio stations. But she refused to be intimidated by such scare tactics, despite the real danger of alienating her fan base and threatening her newfound financial security. She fired back with a song about divorce, another taboo in the Christian South of the time. This coal miner's daughter refused to give up her integrity, regardless of the cost.

I've always defined integrity as when my inside and outside match—when I experience no gap between how I feel on the inside and how I act on the outside. It's a practice, not a destination, to live into life as it actually shows up, not as I simply imagine it.

Integrity is hard work, at least for me. Despite my commitment to it, over and over I find myself saying or doing things that make my life easier, not because they are a reflection of my deepest held beliefs or values. I profess kindness and ignore suffering all the time in the form of homeless people on the street. I espouse antimaterialism while seeking to increase my bank account. The gap doesn't feel good, but at least when I experience the discomfort, I am reminded of my goal. And when I do choose the path of integrity, even when it's difficult, I experience a sense of greater satisfaction with myself and my life.

Integrity creates happiness because it requires us to tell ourselves the truth about what matters to us, which becomes a compass for all the decisions of our lives. Here's how Suze Orman puts it: "In my experience, most people are unhappy because they aren't being truthful with themselves. Being truthful with yourself plugs you into your inner power. Whether it's your relationship with money or with a partner, you aren't going to be content or successful until you are connected to your heart and operating with all your energy. And that requires a commitment to a life based on honesty in every aspect. If you can pull that off, it's virtually impossible not to be happy."

What Orman is saying is that integrity allows us to be wholehearted, undivided, which by itself creates happiness. We're not pulled in a thousand directions, we're not hiding from ourselves and thus have greater strength and capacity to create what we want: a happier relationship, greater financial peace of mind, a better job. But it is not only because of the results we get that integrity creates happiness. It's also because such wholeheartedness produces a sense of peace of mind, an experience of personal harmony.

Loretta Lynn's acts of integrity had happy consequences. The most visible to the outside world was that her bold stances brought her to the attention of a much wider listening audience, so that by the 1980s she was ranked by the *Ladies' Home Journal* as one of the one hundred most admired women in the world.

If you are not as happy day to day as you would like, perhaps you need to do an integrity check. Where are you not being totally truthful with yourself? Where are you hiding from or fooling yourself? Without beating yourself up, take fifteen minutes to take an honest look at your life. Don't try to make an exhaustive list of all your inconsistencies. Whatever comes up first is most likely what you need to begin working on. What one action can you take to begin to bring yourself into alignment? I've made a commitment to smile or say hello to everyone who crosses my path so that I can feel I am being kinder to others, as I want to be. When I notice I haven't done it, again, I simply recommit to doing it, without beating myself up.

And remember—none of us can be as pure as we might want. We need to have compassion for our humanness as we seek to bring ourselves into integrity.

49

Stretch Yourself

"The truth is that all of us attain the greatest success and happiness possible in this life whenever we use our native capacities to their greatest extent."

—*Dr. Smiley Blanton*

Jack is a senior executive in a large corporation. He asked me to work with him because he felt burned out. At first, I encouraged him to take some vacation time, to exercise, to go home earlier. He did that, but he still felt dead at work. Then I read a book called *The Power of Full Engagement* by Jim Loehr and Tony Schwartz. In it, they argue that a high-performance life is really about having strategies for mental, physical, emotional, and spiritual extension, where you stretch yourself beyond your previous capacity, and recovery, where you lay off and rejuvenate.

When Jack and I thought about it, his problem was not that he wasn't recovering, but that mentally he wasn't being stretched *enough*. He needed a greater work challenge, not more time off. He was slated to become head of his division, but simply continuing to climb that particular ladder would not allow him to grow enough. So he did what to others made no sense—he asked to be moved to another division, which meant that he would not get a promotion right away. But it also meant that he would have "a whole new pond to play in," as he put it, and a new area to learn about. From that moment on, Jack's whole demeanor changed. Each week he came to our calls energized. "Even though I sometimes wonder what the hell I'm doing," he confided, "most of the time I'm having so much fun."

If we look at what the research on happiness says, Jack's story makes sense. Happiness comes not only from moment-to-moment enjoyment of life, but also from the sense of satisfaction and flow that arises when we are using our capacities to their fullest. Our bodies, minds, and spirits are made to be worked. Otherwise, we feel stale. Think of it like this—imagine I gave you a fancy red Ferrari, but all you used it for was to go up and down your driveway all day. It would soon lose its luster. Your being, your essence, is way more magnificent than a Ferrari, and it wants to fly down the highway of life.

That was certainly true for me. I spent twenty-five years as an editor and loved every minute. Until one day I didn't love it anymore, and no amount of time off helped. After floundering for a while, I realized that it was time to do something else. I needed to use my capacities in a different way.

If you don't feel as happy as you would like, maybe it's time to ask yourself one simple question: *Where do I need to stretch so that I feel excited to be alive?* Is it mentally, like Fred, by learning something new or taking on a new job? Is it physically by training for a 10k race or committing to working out three times a week? Is it emotionally by learning new habits or relationship skills? Is it spiritually by exploring your sense of connection to the infinite?

This stretching of ourselves is what William Butler Yeats meant, I believe, when he wrote: "Happiness is neither virtue nor pleasure nor this thing nor that but simply growth. We are happy when we are growing."

50

Cultivate Sensibility

"People from a planet without flowers would think we must be mad with joy the whole time to have such things about us."

—*Iris Murdoch*

This morning I went outside before starting to write. The air was still and sweet, the sun warm and bright on my skin, the trees shimmering in the sunlight. It was quiet— no street or traffic noise. The gray titmice who built a nest in the birdhouse Ana made were feeding their babies. A blue damselfly flitted by. An ordinary, extraordinary summer morning. The only thing different from thousands of other mornings in my life was that I was noticing it.

How many wonderful ordinary moments of our lives do we pass by, full of what we must do next or worried about something that just happened? The world is full of miracles for our five senses if we just open ourselves to receive them. The trick is to look with fresh eyes, hear with new ears. When we do, we come alive again to the wonders all around us—the slant of light on the skyscraper, the smell of hot asphalt as the rain hits the pavement, the sparkle of a stranger's smile—and we feel an uplift of emotion. We touch the sheer joy of being alive.

This uplift is available, free, with no expiration date in every moment of our existence. We can tap into it anywhere, anytime if we but tune in to the world around us. The romantic poets called this capacity *sensibility,* says poet David Whyte, "the power of appreciation for *things as they are.*"

That last phrase—things as they are—is key. I used to believe that I could not enjoy the beauties of life unless all of my life was squared away. Then I began to read and listen to Thich Nhat Hanh, who lived through the terrors of the Vietnamese war. He speaks a lot about the beauty of the world. How can he feel that way when the orphanage he founded was bombed, all his friends and family killed? How can he be so happy now when he is banned from his country? These were questions Westerners kept asking this serenely radiant being. "Joy is something which is born when we recognize what is beautiful and in good condition," he once said. "I nourish myself with peace, with joy, for the sake of my ancestors," he explained, "for the sake of my children and their children... When you are happy you have something to share. When you are happy, you can make people around you happy."

When we take time to appreciate the miracles around us, we are better equipped to handle what life dishes out, good or bad. Enjoying the flowers on the way to the office will not detract from your capacity to work hard when you get there. But it may give you the buoyancy to better handle the problems that hit when you walk in the door. And if the only reward is that for a few moments you felt great, isn't that reward enough?

When you wake up, before you go to sleep, on the way to and from work, take a few moments to look around with fresh eyes. Let yourself really take in the extraordinary world that is all around you. As the wise teenager Anne Frank wrote while hiding in an attic from the Nazis, "Think of all the beauty still left around you and be happy."

51

Take the Actions You Can

"We have to believe in free will.
We've got no choice."

—*Isaac Bashevis Singer*

In his book *The Pursuit of Happiness*, American social psychologist David G. Myers tells of meeting a black South African pastor back in the days of apartheid. Myers asked him "if his year-long visit in my community had changed him. He replied that what surprised him, and changed his consciousness, was not the affluence but the sense of control over his own life. 'Having grown up poor, believing that money would buy happiness, I'm no longer convinced. Here in America I've seen rich people who have money and all it buys, but who are troubled and unhappy. I'm more impressed by your freedom. Here when I see police officers I don't have to worry what they might do to me. When I return to South Africa, I will remember what liberty feels like.'"

There has been a great deal of research into the relationship between a sense of control and happiness. Psychologists differentiate between those who think they have power over their lives, which they call an internal locus of control, and those who think their lives are controlled by others, which they call an external locus of control. People with an internal locus of control tend to deal more effectively with stress, achieve more in school and work, and report greater happiness. In fact, quotes Myers, researcher Angus Campbell of the University of Michigan, referring to a nationwide study, discovered that "having a strong sense of controlling one's life is a more dependable predictor of positive feelings of well-being than any of the objective conditions of life we've considered."

George Bernard Shaw said it more poetically: "Hell is to drift. Heaven is to steer." Unless we feel we have the power to take the actions we need in our lives, we will not be happy. Through repeated early trauma, some of us develop "learned helplessness," feelings of apathy, resignation, and paralysis that serve like a self-fulfilling prophecy: The more we feel we can't make a difference, the greater our sense of helplessness; the greater the sense of helplessness, the less action we take to change our circumstances.

But we can break the cycle. We do it in two ways. First, by noticing where we are free rather than where we are stuck. For instance, if you are having trouble getting pregnant, you can focus on the fact that it is out of your control. Or you can decide to get help from the sophisticated medical techniques now available, adopt a baby, or take the opportunity of childlessness to travel or to find children— nephews, nieces, neighbors—to connect to.

Second, we can set manageable goals for ourselves so that we are taking action on behalf of what we want despite the obstacles. An immigrant friend worked in the food service industry. He didn't like it, but because he had never been to college, it was the only job available to him. He decided to get a college degree. Because he couldn't afford to stop working, he went to night school for ten years to learn computer science. He now makes a hefty salary and loves his work.

What actions do you need to take to increase your happiness? If you feel you have no control over the difficulties of your life, ask others to help you see where you are free. What goals can you set to make a dream come true? If the goal feels daunting, how can you break it down into small steps? What kind of support might you need? Where can you find it?

Liz Murray, a guest on *Oprah,* put it this way: "What if I woke up and every single day I did everything within my ability during that day to change my life? What could happen in just a month, a year? What would be different about my life?" The more you make positive effort toward what you want, the happier you'll be.

52

Make Someone Else Happy

"Happiness is a perfume which you
cannot pour on others without getting
a few drops on yourself."

—*Louis L. Mann*

I wanted to thank someone who had been kind to me. So I sent a bouquet of roses to her office. When ordering, I found out that peach roses stand for appreciation, so I delighted in sending an extra, nonverbal message. I imagined what a surprise they would be, which pleased me even more.

Recently I was asked why, when you think of the perfect gift for someone else, it feels so good. That got me thinking that one of the best ways to activate our own happiness on a daily basis is by looking for simple ways to bring joy to others. It makes us feel great too.

The reason is because we experience something I've never heard spoken of in Western culture. I've just finished reading over fifty books on happiness, and only one mentions it! Buddhists call it *mudita*—sympathetic joy. It's an upswelling of the heart at the happiness or joy of someone else.

Sympathetic joy is the opposite of envy. It's one of the reasons why giving, when it comes from a genuine feeling of overflow—wanting to bring happiness or pleasure to someone else rather than from a sense of obligation—feels so good. We experience in ourselves the good feelings of the other person.

Actually, the giver gets a double whammy of happiness—anticipatory joy in thinking of how the person is going to feel, as well as the actual moment when he or she receives the gift. Sympathetic joy is such a wonderful feeling that you don't even have to be there when the person receives the gift to feel great. That's what's behind random acts of kindness, for instance—just thinking about how the person in the car behind you at the tollbooth is going to feel when you pay her toll gives you a bolt of pleasure. That's what Walt Whitman meant when he said, "The gift is to the giver and comes back most to him—it cannot fail."

You don't have to buy elaborate gifts or spend a lot of time or effort. You can get the boost from giving to others in many ways: surprises to children in the form of a love note in their lunch boxes, a flower from your garden on a coworker's desk, the perfect card for a friend.

Have you ever been with someone who, when they do you a courtesy and you offer thanks, says, "My pleasure"? It truly is a pleasure to spread kindness, even if it's simply holding the door for someone who is struggling with a load of packages.

Try an experiment. Commit to giving something, no matter how small, every day for a week. A kind word, a smile to someone you know is going through tough times, an offer to mentor a young colleague, an e-mail out of the blue thanking someone for the impact he's had on your life. Even if you don't feel great, do it anyway for a week and notice what effect it has. Do you feel more joyful, more connected to others, and happy to be alive?

This truly is one of the easiest, most powerful ways to experience joy every day. Here's how Count Maurice Maeterlinck puts it: "Above all let us not forget that an act of goodness is an act of happiness."

53

What Are You Waiting For?

Always we hope
Someone else has the answer,
Some other place it will be better,
Some other time
It will all turn out.

This is it.
No one else has the answer.
No other place will be better,
And it has already turned out.

—Lao Tzu

I used to belong to the happiness-is-right-around-the-corner-as-soon-as-I _____(fill in the blank) school of living. Happiness was some state of existence I would reach as soon as certain things happened: as soon as I left home, as soon as I had some money, as soon as my husband gets a job.

I clearly remember falling in love at age twenty-five with a man with two kids, aged two and six months, and thinking to myself, *well, we can be happy after the kids are grown. It's only eighteen more years.* (Honestly!) And then I proceeded to endure my sentence of stepparent as best I could, holding out for the mythical time when I would be free to be happy.

Needless to say, that day never came. He left me when the youngest was fourteen, which taught me many things, one of the most important being that it never makes sense to defer happiness. In learning from that event, I became committed to happiness, as Walt Whitman put it, "not in another place, but this place... not for another hour, but this hour." I refuse to wait anymore for a payoff that may never materialize.

Can you choose to be happy this very minute? With the floor unmopped, the conflict with your spouse or child unresolved, the big questions of your life unanswered? Without the future guaranteed?

That's what life is really calling us to do, because the only day when it's all sewn up is the day of your death. Until then, we're called upon to enjoy the dance with life in all its messiness and incompleteness.

As I sit here in front of the computer, it's the Fourth of July. Outside my window, family and friends are sitting around the pool and splashing in the water. I am inside, writing about happiness. In the past, I would have endured the work in order to finally get to the pool, perhaps feeling sorry for myself that I was working while others were lounging. Now, because I want to enjoy all my moments, I am aware of how great it feels to be using my mind for a purpose I deem worthy as well as how wonderful it will feel to slide into the water in a few hours. And I am happy that those I care about are enjoying themselves. As a consequence, I am happy with the way my life is right in this moment, rather than wishing or hoping for some other kind of moment to be occurring.

Recently I read *All I Really Need to Know I Learned in Kindergarten* for the first time. In it, Robert Fulghum tells a story I absolutely love. When he was a minister, he was always flabbergasted when someone from his flock would come for spiritual counseling, saying, "The doctors told me I have only a limited time to live." Fulghum confesses that he always wanted to shout, *"What?* You didn't know? You had to pay a doctor to tell you—at your age? Where were you the week in kindergarten when you got the little cup with the cotton and water and seed? Life happened— remember? A plant grew up and the roots grew down. A miracle. And then a few days later the plant was dead... The idea was for us to have the whole picture right from the beginning. Life-and-death. Lifedeath. One event. One short event. Don't forget."

This is it—your one and only short life. How shall you live so that you enjoy it absolutely as much as possible?

IV

TWENTY-TWO INSTANT
HAPPINESS BOOSTERS

"If ye know these things, happy
are ye if ye do them."

—*John 13:17*

1. What has brought you the most happiness in your life? What were you doing? Noting when and how you experience happiness helps you, like a heat-seeking missile, go toward it more.

2. Do an appreciation circle. It takes only a few moments, and it's a great spreader of happiness. You can do it with family or coworkers, any group of people who know one another fairly well. Choose one person as the focus. Then everyone else, as they feel moved, speaks of what they appreciate about that person. When everyone who wants to has spoken, choose another person until everyone has received appreciation. There are only four rules:

    (1) Remarks must be positive (no sarcasm or back-handed compliments).

    (2) No cross talk—no one else may speak when someone is talking.

    (3) No one has to talk if he or she doesn't want to.

    (4) The focus person says nothing. This may be a challenge, for we tend to want to deflect or minimize compliments. But try to take them in, as much as you can allow yourself.

3. Practice accepting others as they are. Try it just for today. When you notice yourself judging someone as bad (the screaming child, the insensitive clerk), pause, take a breath, and say to yourself, "They want to be happy just as I do. They're doing the best they can."

4. Find yourself stuck in worry mode? Figure out if you can do something about it—like planning for the pre-

sentation you have to give—or if it's out of your control, like waiting for test results. If there is something you can do, great—do it. If not, make a list of all the possible *good* outcomes.

5. At the beginning of January, when you get a new appointment book or are setting up your Outlook for the year, randomly select six days sprinkled throughout the year and put a special symbol on them—a sticker, a star, whatever. Then, when you come to them during the year, give yourself a treat. This will bring you happiness sevenfold—the six treats and the smile it brings now in anticipation of what's to come.

6. Become aware of your negative mental habits. Here's a practice from Wayne Muller. When something goes wrong, say to yourself, *It's just as I've always known:* _____. What phrase leaps in to fill the blank? Most of us have an unconscious negative thought that we use to keep ourselves unhappy. Mine is: "I'm going to end up as a bag lady on the street." Steve's is: "Nothing good ever happens to me." Once you figure out what yours is, practice saying it a few times in different voice tones—angry, sad, teasing. The more you bring this thought into awareness, the less effect it will have.

7. Make or buy a bouquet. Researchers at Rutgers found that flowers put a genuine smile on 100 percent of recipients' faces. They don't know why flowers create happiness, but those receiving them reported less stress, sadness, and anxiety and a greater sense of well-being.

8. What music are you listening to? What books are you reading? Are you sinking into a pit of gloom by contagion? Research has shown that our moods are greatly influenced by what we listen to and read. When I was in my twenties and seeing a therapist for my unhappiness, she asked me what I was reading. "Sylvia Plath," I responded. "Put that away," she ordered, "and read something uplifting. And no Leonard Cohen music either!" She "prescribed" a collection of stories of pioneer women who withstood all odds. Guess what? I felt better instantly.

9. Make a list of what Dawna Markova, author of *I Will Not Die an Unlived Life,* calls "life-cherishing forces," those relationships, places, pets, and experiences that make your life worth living. Then when you're feeling down, take out the list and read it out loud.

10. Remember the bad old days. We often wax nostalgic about the past, conveniently forgetting all that was difficult or challenging. Novelist Milan Kundera called this tendency "the unbearable lightness of being." It's a terrible happiness killer. In one experiment, people who wrote about a wonderful time in their past were significantly less satisfied with their present life, while those who wrote about a difficult time were much more content now. So when you find yourself strolling down memory lane, be sure to recall what was hard about it too.

11. Happiness being destroyed by having eyes bigger than your wallet? Get yourself out of temptation's way. Avoid the mall, get yourself off catalog mailing lists. What you don't see, you won't be tempted to purchase.

12. Doesn't it feel great to set a goal and accomplish it? What's something that you've been procrastinating about that would give you a great sense of satisfaction

to finally do? Clean out the garage? Clear your desk at work? Ask yourself, what would bring me happiness to accomplish? Pick something that's realistic and set a deadline for yourself.

13. At the end of the day—driving home from work, at dinner with your family, just before you go to sleep, whatever works for you—ask yourself three questions:

    (1) What am I thankful for today?

    (2) What do I feel satisfied about?

    (3) What did I enjoy doing today?

14. An ancient Buddhist list offers four ways to experience physical joy or exhilaration:

    (1) eating;

    (2) sleeping;

    (3) meditating;

    (4) taking care of your body through bathing, grooming, moving.

    You can probably think of a fifth—it was most likely celibates who came up with the list.

15. Suffering from pain, mental or physical? Thinking of it as *the* pain rather than *my* pain helps create a bit of breathing room. From that place you can start to experience that you are more than the pain, for you are also the one observing it. You are like the blue sky with clouds—the pain—blowing past. The clouds may come and go, but the sky is eternal. The more you can rest in big-sky mind, expanding around the pain rather than tightening against it or trying to deny it, the more it becomes possible to bear.

16. If you are someone who tends to postpone happiness until some event, try this idea from *Happiness Is Free*: "Make a list of persons, places, things, and accomplishments or situations that you believe will make you happy... With every item on your list, ask yourself: 'Could I let go of wanting to get happiness from (your item) and allow myself to rest as the happiness I already am?...' We are postponing happiness most of the time without being aware of it... As you let go of postponing happiness in these ways, you will discover a deepening sense of happiness that will be with you all the time enhancing all the things that you used to think you required in order to be happy."

17. Relish what you have. I learned this one from my daughter. Since very young, Ana has always taken great pleasure in her possessions. Recently I bought her a bathrobe, her first. This morning she came in wearing it. "Doesn't it look great?" she said. "Look at the flowers on the sleeves. And the beautiful purple color. And the fuzzy fabric feels so good! It even smells nice." Through all her senses, she thoroughly enjoys what she has. Consequently, the smallest things make her happy. Interestingly, this appreciation also allows her to detach when the object is lost, broken, or used up—she has so thoroughly enjoyed it that she's not sad when something disappears. Really enjoying your possessions helps you not only feel the abundance in your life, it's one of the best ways to counteract the "gimme hole," that sense of emptiness that we tend to want to fill with more, more, more.

18. Are you having fun yet? What do you do to play? We all need the exuberant energy of play in our lives. I hate games, but love to dance wildly; that's how I play. Fold some play into your life on a daily basis: tennis,

chess, loud singing. Try an improv class, dress up with your kids, rock climbing—whatever is fun for you.

19. Take a joy break instead of a coffee break. When you find yourself bored or snippy at work or home, go into the bathroom and lock the door. For three minutes, think of something that makes you really happy: lying on a beach in Hawaii, laughing with your best friend, whatever gives you joy. Bring it to mind as vividly as possible: really see, feel, hear yourself in it. Since the brain doesn't differentiate from vivid imaginings and actually doing something, you'll get a rush of good feelings as if you were experiencing it right now.

20. When you find yourself mired in regret about a choice you've made, remember this little slogan from Dottie Gandy's and Marsha Clark's book *Choose!:* "There is no such thing as a bad choice; there is only a next choice." You might even want to make a card with this saying and post it somewhere you can see if often.

21. I once got an e-mail from a guy named Larry who wrote: "I want people to be happier after I come into a room than before." What if you adopted Larry's attitude? How would you treat those you meet as you go through your day? Give it a try and see what a joy it is to be a joy!

22. When you finish something, celebrate as much as you would have bemoaned not finishing. When someone does something that pleases you, rejoice as much as you would have been angry if they had done something annoying. When you find something you've been looking for, celebrate as much as you would have been upset if you hadn't found it. In other words, take every chance you have to revel in the good things that happen to you. Celebration itself is a creator of joy.

V
LOVING YOUR LIFE

"Sit. Feast on your life."

—*Derek Walcott*

Jean-Dominique Bauby was the editor in chief of the fashion magazine *Elle*. At age forty-three, he had a stroke and lapsed into a three-week coma. When he awoke, he discovered he had locked-in syndrome, a condition in which he was mentally undamaged and had normal body sensations, but was totally paralyzed with the exception of being able to blink his left eye. To communicate, he developed a code in which he blinked the letters of the alphabet and, in this laborious way, dictated a 114-page book called *The Diving Bell and the Butterfly*, which he called his "bedridden travel notes." The title came from Bauby's sense of his experience, which was that while his body felt trapped in a diving bell, his mind was free to float like a butterfly. He lived two years, just long enough to create this remarkable chronicle and see it published in France, dying just two days after its release.

His life is proof of a person's capacity to create meaning—through the act of blinking this extraordinary memoir—and find happiness, even occasions for joy, in the midst of tragedy. Deprived of the capacity to eat and kept alive through intravenous fluids, he learns "the art of simmering memories... I treat myself to a dozen snails... or else I savor a simple soft-boiled egg with fingers of toast and lightly salted butter. What a banquet! The yolk flows warmly over my palate and down my throat. And indigestion is never a problem. Naturally I use the finest ingredients: the freshest vegetables, fish straight from the water, the most delicately marbled meat. Everything must be done right." He's no Pollyanna, however: "To keep my mind sharp, to avoid descending into resigned indifference, I maintain a level of resentment and anger, neither too much nor too little, just as a pressure cooker has a safety valve to keep it from exploding."

Warm, sad, wry, Bauby's book is ultimately about his love of life, his life. And that's ultimately what happiness is all about. Inside each of us is the awareness, as David Whyte describes it, "that somewhere at the center of life is something ineffably and unalterably right and good, and that this 'rightness' can be discovered." What Bauby proved is that we can all tap into it, no matter our circumstances.

Canadian philosopher Mark Kingwell says that when we consider happiness, what we are really asking is: "Am I living a life that I judge worth living?" Happiness, he notes, is "the ability to reflect on one's life and find it worthwhile—to see it as satisfactory."

Each of us finds worth in a unique combination of ways, shapes, and forms—through purpose in work, love of friends and family, losing ourselves in the flow of creativity, gratitude, generosity, and kindness to others, simple pleasures, using our talents on behalf of our values. And only we can judge whether it adds up to a worthwhile life. And the judging, I've come to see, is not a mental reckoning at some point in the far distant future when we're called upon to justify our existence, but a felt experience of pleasure, satisfaction, and fulfillment in the here and now that we activate, like Bauby, through the moment-to-moment embracing of our life as it is, in all its human messiness and miraculousness. Through treasuring our normal days, we create days worth treasuring.

Buddhism encourages us to embrace our lives with this kind of passion and vigor by reminding us of the preciousness of our incarnation—that simply to be alive is by itself an occasion for happiness. But this understanding permeates many other traditions: "Be happy while you're living," says a Scottish proverb, "for you're a long time dead." When we awaken to the miracle of existence, every day becomes an occasion to rejoice, and happiness flows naturally. The French writer Colette once proclaimed: "What a wonderful life I've had! I only wish I'd realized it sooner."

How can you, can I, live so that we don't have to say a similar thing? Every single day, we are given another twenty-four hours to notice our wonderful life and to do what we can with what we have to savor it.

In ancient Egypt, there was a belief that the god Osiris greets the dead with two questions: Did you bring joy? Did you find joy? I want to live each day so that I can answer with a resounding yes. If not to ensure a spot in heaven, at least so that I will know deep in my bones that I have honored the life I've been given and contributed to an uplift in human hearts. What else are we here for?

May you find joy in your ordinary days and may you bring joy to others through the beauty of your heart, mind, and spirit.

Yes
It could happen any time, tornado,
Earthquake, Armageddon. It could happen.
Or sunshine, love, salvation.

It could, you know. That's why we wake
And look out—no guarantees
in this life.

But some bonuses, like morning,
like right now, like noon,
like evening.

     —William Stafford

Acknowledgments

A bow of infinite respect and boundless gratitude to the happiness teachers whom I've apprenticed with over the years: Dawna Markova, Daphne Rose Kingma, Ana Li McIlraith, Donald McIlraith, Sylvia Boorstein, Jack Kornfield, Thich Nhat Hanh, Vincent Ryan, Charon Scott, Tami Rush; the Silver Springs sangha who shared their unpublished manuscript on everyday Buddhism; and the many authors throughout the ages who have written on this primary topic, especially Stella Resnick, whose book *The Pleasure Zone* helped launch me consciously on the quest to enjoy my life.

Special thanks to Laura Matthews at *Good Housekeeping*, for assigning me an article on this topic—you are this book's fairy godmother. A bouquet of appreciation to Kathy Cordova for the title and Heather McArthur for giving me structural advice under adverse circumstances.

Endless gratitude to book midwives Debra Goldstein, for her belief in me, and Kris Puopolo, for the opportunity to spend time contemplating happiness—what an incredible privilege. Thanks, too, to all the other thoughtful hearts and hands at The Creative Culture and Broadway Books, including Nicole Diamond Austin and Marianne Naples,

Beth Haymaker, and Laura Pillar. Thanks to Emily Miles and Leslie Rossman of Open Book, my faithful publicists over the years, for helping get my work out there.

A great whoop of appreciation to Dave Peck, who helped me understand flow, particularly as it is experienced in the body, and gave me the words to describe it.

Thanks as well to all my clients and friends who share the journey with me and appear here in disguised form to protect their confidentiality; to my sister Stephanie for being such a source of happiness to me; and to my work colleagues Robin Rankin, Angie McArthur, Dave Peck, Andy Bryner, and Dawna Markova, who so graciously support everything I do. My dear writing companion Dawna especially helped with the conception of the book and with many of the practices.

Finally, I give thanks also for all the lessons in my life, the painful ones as well as those I enjoyed learning. I know I am happier for all that I have grown from, the good and the bad.

Bibliography

Argyle, Michael. *The Psychology of Happiness*. East Sussex, Great Britain: Routledge, 2001.

Baird, David. *A Thousand Paths to Happiness*. London: MQ Publications Limited, 2000.

Baker, Dan, Ph.D. *What Happy People Know*. New York: Rodale, 2003.

Baran, Josh. *365 Nirvana Here and Now*. London: Element, 2003.

Bauby, Jean-Dominique. *The Diving Bell and the Butterfly*. New York: Vintage, 1998.

Burns, David D., M.D. *The Feeling Good Handbook*. New York: Plume, 1990, 1999.

www.catholicworker.org.

Chetkin, Len. *100 Thoughts that Lead to Happiness*. Charlottesville, VA: Hampton Roads Publishing Company, 2002.

Cushnir, Howard Raphael. *Unconditional Bliss*. Wheaton, IL: Quest Books, 2000.

The Dalai Lama and Howard C. Cutler, M.D. *The Art of Happiness*. New York: Riverhead, 1998.

Dwoskin, Hale, and Lester Levenson. *Happiness Is Free and It's Easier than You Think*. Sedona, AZ: Sedona Training Associates, 2001.

Ellsberg, Robert. *The Saints' Guide to Happiness*. New York: North Point Press, 2003.

Foster, Rick, and Greg Hicks. *How We Choose to Be Happy*. New York: G. P. Putnam's Sons, 1999.

Fulghum, Robert. *All I Really Need to Know I Learned in Kindergarten*. New York: Ballantine Books, 2003.

Goleman, Daniel, Richard Boyatzis, and Annie McKee. *The Art of Happiness at Work*. New York: Riverhead, 2003.

———. *Primal Leadership*. Boston: Harvard Business School Press, 2002.

Johnson, Robert, and Jerry M. Ruhl. *Contentment*. San Francisco: HarperSanFrancisco, 1999.

Kast, Verena. *Joy, Inspiration and Hope*. Texas: Texas A&M University Press, 1991.

Kehoe, John. *The Practice of Happiness*. Vancouver, BC: Zoetic, 1999.

Kingwell, Mark. *In Pursuit of Happiness*. New York: Crown Publishers, 1998.

Loehr, Jim, and Tony Schwartz. *The Power of Full Engagement*. New York: Free Press, 2003.

Ludema, James D. "From Deficit Discourse to Vocabularies of Hope: The Power of Appreciation." *Appreciative Inquiry: An Emerging Direction for Organization Development*, David L. Cooperrider, Peter F. Sorensen, Jr., Therese F. Yaeger, and Diana Whitney, editors. Champaign, IL: Stipes Publishing, 2001.

Lykken, Dr. David. *Happiness*. New York: St. Martin Griffin, 1999.

The Monks of New Skete. *In the Spirit of Happiness*. Boston: Little, Brown, 1999.

Myers, David G., Ph.D. *The Pursuit of Happiness*. New York: Avon, 1992.

Osho. *Joy*. New York: St. Martin's Press, 2004.

Peck, M. Scott, M.D. *Abounding Happiness.* Kansas City, MO: Andrews McMeel Publishing, 2003.

Pieper, Josef. *Happiness & Contemplation.* South Bend, IN: St. Augustine's Press, 1979.

Powell, John. *Happiness Is an Inside Job.* Allen, TX: Thomas More, 1989, 1999.

Prager, Dennis. *Happiness Is a Serious Problem.* New York: ReganBooks, 1998.

Resnick, Stella. *The Pleasure Zone.* Berkeley, CA: Conari Press, 1997.

Russell, Bertrand. *The Conquest of Happiness.* New York: Liveright, 1930.

Schwartz, Barry. *The Paradox of Choice.* New York: HarperCollins, 2004.

Seligman, Martin. *Authentic Happiness.* New York: Free Press, 2002.

Stoddard, Alexandra. *Choosing Happiness.* New York: HarperResource, 2002.

Templeton, John Marks. *The Templeton Plan.* As told to James Ellison. New York: HarperPaperbacks, 1987.

Thase, Michael E., M.D., and Susan S. Lang. *Beating the Blues.* New York: Oxford University Press, 2004.

Urban, Hal. *Positive Words, Powerful Results.* New York: Fireside, 2004.

Vaughan, Susan C., M.D. *Half Empty, Half Full.* New York: Harcourt, 2000.

Whyte, David. *The Heart Aroused.* New York: Currency/Doubleday, 2002.

Zerah, Aaron. *Every Day Is a Blessing.* New York: Warner Books, 2002.

About the Author

M.J. Ryan is one of the creators of *The New York Times* bestselling *Random Acts of Kindness* and the author of *How to Survive Change... You Didn't Ask For, The Power of Patience,* and *Attitudes of Gratitude,* among other titles. She is a contributing editor to *Health.com* and *Good Housekeeping* and has appeared on *The Today Show,* CNN, and hundreds of radio programs. Visit her at *www. mj-ryan.com.*

Mango Publishing, established in 2014, publishes an eclectic list of books by diverse authors—both new and established voices—on topics ranging from business, personal growth, women's empowerment, LGBTQ studies, health, and spirituality to history, popular culture, time management, decluttering, lifestyle, mental wellness, aging, and sustainable living. We were recently named 2019 and 2020's #1 fastest-growing independent publisher by *Publishers Weekly*. Our success is driven by our main goal, which is to publish high-quality books that will entertain readers as well as make a positive difference in their lives.

Our readers are our most important resource; we value your input, suggestions, and ideas. We'd love to hear from you—after all, we are publishing books for you!

Please stay in touch with us and follow us at:
  Facebook: Mango Publishing
  Twitter: @MangoPublishing
  Instagram: @MangoPublishing
  LinkedIn: Mango Publishing
  Pinterest: Mango Publishing
  Newsletter: mangopublishinggroup.com/newsletter

Join us on Mango's journey to reinvent publishing, one book at a time.

CPSIA information can be obtained
at www.ICGtesting.com
Printed in the USA
LVHW040043300422
717571LV00019B/1375